Toxic Love

SHADOWED DESIRES: LOYALTY, LOVE, AND DECEPTION

Kathy Lou Waskett

Explora Books
700 – 838 West Hastings St. Vancouver, BC V6C 0A6
www.explorabooks.com
Phone: (604) 330 67951

Published by Explora Books 2024

ISBN: 978-1-9983-9401-2 (e)

Table of Contents

Foreword i

Introduction v

Chapter 1...1

    Ricardo's Story ....

Chapter 2...7

    Marta ....

Chapter 3...11

    Glenda ....

Chapter 4...15

Chapter 5...19

    Vladimir and Marta ....

Chapter 6...21

    Toxic Love..

Chapter 7...27

Chapter 8...31

Chapter 9...35

Chapter 10...41

    Day of the Wolf ....

Chapter 11 47

Chapter 12 51

Chapter 13 59

Chapter 14 67

Chapter 15 69

Chapter 16 79

Chapter 17 83

Chapter 18 87

Chapter 19 91

Chapter 20 95

Chapter 21 99

Chapter 22 107

Chapter 23 111

Chapter 24 115

Chapter 25 119

Chapter 26 123

Chapter 27 127

Chapter 28 131

Chapter 29 135

Chapter 30 143

Chapter 31 147

Chapter 32 155

Chapter 33 167

Foreword

There are many forms of toxic love. One form is the kind where you love someone who can hurt or destroy you.

Another kind is what you do to yourself to make the pain go away. These types of pain are written about frequently in dramas, tabloids, and self-help books. One type of toxic love is rarely written about. It is a love for people over the Internet.

You can't look in their eyes. You don't know their character or motives. They will tell you the things you want to hear. They will find out about your passions, interests, dreams, and hopes. They will let you talk about your day. They will seem like your best friend. They make you believe that they will always love you. All you have to do is give your money, bank account information, or resources. They will make it up to you.

Sadly, people will do this because they want to believe there are still honest and decent people. They are lonely or want to get rich quickly. The end result is devastating and can lead to bankruptcy, despair, and loss of everything for which they have worked. Because victims allow the scammer into their accounts, they have to pick up the pieces. There are many Internet scams out there to get people's money.

One of the saddest is where someone is hoping to find love and is deceived online. The scammer's motive is to get money, property, or something else that is valuable to the person he or she is contacting. What is sad is that most of the victims do this willingly. They are hoping for someone or something better than what they have.

This is a story that deals with one of those situations. I hope that you enjoy the story and that you will learn from our characters what this kind of love can do. I have included Marta's and Ricardo's songs at the end. Their songs speak of passion and romance.

The boss is like the puppeteer, pulling Ricardo's strings and telling him what to do. Ricardo's heart tells him to help others. His wallet tells him to get money anyway he can. The boss has been a father to Ricardo since he was very young. However, the reason he cared for Ricardo was to train him. He wanted Ricardo to take up the business for him.

Vladimir is in love with Marta, but she is not in love with him. This caused Vladimir to want Ricardo out of the way. Ricardo has to make a decision. Will he choose the love of his life? Marta? Or will Glenda's unconditional love win out? How will Ricardo help Katie, Edward's wife, to get away from Edward? Will Katie survive in the midst of Edward's rampages? The Headlines say about Ricardo that he is the shadow in the night.

The man without a face. A shadow in its place. No one will recognize your disguise. You come from far and near. One thing is very clear. No one will know you when you pass by. The man walks like a shadow in the night!

He is now fighting for the right. He walks like a shadow in the night!

Introduction

Ricardo has an idea of what he wants: money, adventure, good times, and a partnership in the boss's company.

Ricardo meets Marta.

Marta is a beautiful, smart, and talented lady. She has all the qualities that a man would want. He finds out what he was looking for was caring and unconditional love.

However, he had to do what the boss said or he was a dead man. Glenda is soft-spoken, trusting, and sometimes gullible. It is Glenda's trust in his love that causes her to lose everything. Yet, eventually she believes she has gained his love.

The boss is like the puppeteer, pulling Ricardo's strings and telling him what to do. Ricardo's heart tells him to help others. His wallet tells him to get money anyway he can. The boss has been a father to Ricardo since he was very young.

The reason he cared for Ricardo was to train him. He wanted Ricardo to take up the business for him. Vladimir is in love with Marta, but she is not in love with him. This caused Vladimir to want Ricardo out of the way.

Ricardo has to make a decision. Will he choose the love of his life? Marta?

Or will Glenda's unconditional love win out? How will Ricardo help Katie, Edward's wife, to get away from Edward? Will Katie survive in the midst of Edward's rampages?

The Headlines say about Ricardo that he is the shadow in the night. The man without a face. A shadow in its place. No one will recognize your disguise. You come from far and near. One thing is very clear. No one will know you when you pass by.
The man walks like a shadow in the night! He is now fighting for the right. He walks like a shadow in the night!

Chapter 1

Ricardo's Story

My name is Richard. You ask what happened to me. There was a time I was just like you. Young, innocent, unaware of how life's events can change a person. Everything will be beautiful, clean, fresh, and perfect till that one day. Then something completely changes your world, and nothing is the same. I still remember that day. Well, why not? I live it every day in my mind like it was yesterday.

We lived in the Ukraine, and my dad worked at Chernobyl's nuclear plant. I was eight and had friends whose fathers worked at the plant. We lived in the town of Pripyat. Pripyat was built to house workers at the plant. My brother and I went to school in town. Mom was a nurse in the hospital. I watched after my brother Joseph and we helped with the chores.

My brother and I liked to get on the swings and point our feet towards the sky. We pretended we were flying in midair without a net and without anything to stop us reaching our destination. When you are kids, that's what you do. Your imagination gets the best of you and you go with the flow.

I remember seeing the nuclear plant nearby and not thinking much of it because that is where my dad worked. It is where he went to provide for the family. I knew that dad would spend time with us when he could. He was a good dad to us. Mom called Joey and I to eat dinner. She had a setting ready by each paper plate and had lemonade to drink.

Mom made up our plates and dad said a blessing over the food. Joey and I were expected to keep our eyes closed during prayer time. Sometimes we would open one eye and look at each other and giggle about something. Mom would give us the look and we would settle down. Joseph was five at the time and he was always up to mischief. Joey talked about seeing a deer in the forest while we were eating. Normally that would be a happy memory. Dad would share a story and we would start laughing. I would share something that happened at school.

Nothing could prepare our family for what happened at the nuclear plant. No one was told of the radiation or its effects for years to come. Mom and dad sat with us and said we would have to be evacuated because of the radiation

In the air. It was for our safety. Why can't you come with us? I cried out! My dad, Boris, said he had to stay and help with the plant. Anya, my mom, needed to stay at the hospital because she was essential personnel. Momma assured us that Aunt Sophie in London would care for us. Mom and dad would meet us in London when the crisis was over.

We went to school the next day and all seemed normal except that the teachers closed the windows and doors. They issued us iodine tablets. At 2:30p:m, soldiers came and evacuated the whole school and my brother and I ended up in a hostel for the night. 350,000 were evacuated. It was supposed to be for a few days and weeks. Or so we were told. We weren't able to bring anything with us. Our favorite toys, our favorite memories of childhood stayed in our homes. After many moves, we ended up in London with our Aunt Sophie.
She took us in and was very kind to us.

I asked her when we could see our parents. Aunt Sophie started crying. She took out a letter that she received. She held a handkerchief to her eyes. Then she straightened her posture and asked us to sit down.

Your father was a firefighter and he worked over the fires over reactor 4 at Chernobyl nuclear plant. He was exposed to massive amounts of radioactivity. He died four days later after the explosion.

What about mom? Richard, I was hoping that she could join us. However, I just received word that she died from the effects of radiation. She helped so many people. I am so sorry Richard and Joseph.

Aunt Sophie taught us conversational and grammatical English and I was very good at it. I excelled in math and geometry. I became a fighter and made sure that no one would mess with my kid brother or me.

My aunt was not like my real parents. I became angry and bitter because my life had turned upside down. Aunt Sophie did not understand, and I was young and could not explain myself or how I was feeling. I was more like dad because men do not show emotion. They keep their feelings to themselves.

When I was young, all someone had to do was look at me the wrong way and I would beat them up. I was constantly getting into trouble. Joseph became quiet and withdrawn and we didn't play much outside. I had no way to deal with the anger that was fuming within.

One day I was at school and I started thinking about my mom, Anya. I started feeling different. I excused myself from my desk in my classroom and went to the bathroom. I closed the stall door and sat on the toilet. I gasped when I saw my arms and legs look like a shadow. I walked to the sink and looked in the bathroom mirror. But I could not see my hand! I was scared until I thought that I could get back at the kids that had tried to bully me. I wondered if I could control this reaction when it would come over me. I did not know when it would happen or if I could make it start or stop. I went back to the classroom and I was myself again.

At first, disappearing or becoming a shadow became a game to me. My only explanation is that something happened to me when I lived in Pripyat. My reaction to the toxins was becoming a shadow when I became angry or upset. I learned to get out of the house without anyone seeing me. Eventually, I learned how to turn the reaction on and off as I controlled my emotions. The trick was to close my eyes and keep my mind blank from any emotion. I would open my eyes and be myself again.

Joseph had severe asthma and trouble breathing. Aunt Sophie took him regularly to the hospital to get breathing treatments. I helped him with his homework the best I could. I was a quick learner and could speak English fluently.

Kids respected me at school and I had my own gang. That was when the boss met me. It was when he was driving around looking for kids to pick up. I understand now that is what they call child trafficking.

I was on the street, smoking a cigarette, and trying to be cool with my friends. The boss stopped the car, opened his car door and walked over to me.

Hey kid! My name is Edward! How about working for me?

I looked at him and could tell there was something about him that hit my gut. He's not a nice person. I just shrugged the feeling away. Then he became nice and said that he wanted to be my friend. I just laughed it off and said why would I want to work for you?

Edward kept visiting me on the street when I was with my friends. I didn't tell Aunt Sophie because she had other problems. She could no longer house us and informed Joseph and I that we would be living with foster parents. Joseph was still having problems breathing. I felt like the weight of the world was on my shoulders. We moved into a foster home in a nice neighborhood. My new parents started to set rules for me. I wasn't about to be controlled. I ran away.

Edward saw me on the road and offered me a lift. He said that he would take care of me. The boss said that he had other kids working on the street. I would be his favorite.

One day on the job, I started changing again to a shadowy form. The boss saw me change. He said, I knew there was something special about you! From now on, you will be like a son to me. I like being called his son. I became old enough that I was able to choose who was my caregiver and I chose Edward.

I wanted Joseph to join us but Edward said my kid brother was to sick and that he might make everyone else sick. That was the last time I saw my brother or heard from my brother till that message on my answering machine.

Edward adopted me as his own. He changed my named to Ricardo. We would hunt, fish, trap, and camp together. We would work on cars and go out to eat. He took good care of me.

Everything in my life from then on became toxic, and I lost all feelings of remorse or regret. Edward gave me an alias so no one would know who I was. I was named Ricardo for work purposes. Everything that I had trusted and believed had let me down. I became as toxic as the air I breathed in my hometown of Pripyat.

Chapter 2
Marta

Marta was wearing a midi-length black dress, black pump shoes, and a black veiled hat as she stood in front of her son's grave. Her mom, dad, and sister stood beside her to show support.

Marta started crying and calling her son's name. The pastor gave a speech over the grave and talked about how everyone will eventually meet their maker.

Marta was obvious to most of the things the pastor said for all she could think about what her life was over and she would never see her son. Marta's aunt drove into the funeral home parking lot and parked the car.

She walked over to Marta at the graveside and held Marta as she wept bitterly.

"Marta, what are you going to do now? Have you given your future any thought "I have no future. Look at that little boy that is dead right before you. That was my future!

"Would you like to do something to stop the violence and protect the peace?

"What kind of job would that be? I can't work! I don't know what I can do anymore because everything I worked towards is gone." Her aunt said, "It's not gone! You have got to find out what you will be best at and I can't choose that for you."

Marta looked at her aunt through tears but she felt upset that her aunt would even bring up her future at a time like this. "Come and see me in a couple of weeks. Maybe together we can figure out what options you have."

Marta thought about what her aunt said as she threw flowers into her son's grave. "I will get that person who killed my son and I will make him pay for this."

Marta watched as the final dirt was put over the casket and headed to the church reception hall where they were having the bereavement party in honor of her son. "Goodbye Michael. I loved you..."

Marta walked away and walked towards her car. She opened the door, sat down, and gripped the steering wheel. Marta vowed to herself, "This is the last time I will be hurt again. If I can get through this I can get through anything.

Two weeks later she visited her aunt and said that she was interested in joining the police force. Her aunt said, "I don't think I ever told you because it is "Top Secret." "What is it? I thought you worked at a dry cleaners."

That is just a front for what I really do. "I work for the FBI." "Like Mission Impossible? Like Dragnet in the old sitcoms?"

"The sitcoms glamorize being in the FBI. Trust me that there is nothing glamorous about my job. It's very dangerous and not everyone could do the type of job I do and work undercover."

"I was thinking of the police force where cops can stop robbers from hurting people in their homes." "Marta, are you sure you know what you are doing? Have you ever shot a gun?"

"No, but whatever I have to learn I will practice and be the best at it."

Marta got up the next day, got ready, and found out where the police station was. The station was 20 miles away and Marta stopped on the way at a gas station.

A man was pumping gasoline that was in a nice suit and Marta admired how dashing and handsome he looked. The gas was paid for at the self-serve pump and she got 10.00 worth of gasoline.

When Marta went to the register the gentleman was gone. "Hmmm, I wonder if I will ever see him again. Marta walked into the station, asked if any jobs were available, and was handed an application. She filled out the application and handed the paper to the clerk. The clerk's eyes looked interested at Marta's application. She said, "Don't be surprised if you hear from us soon!"

"Thank you!," said Marta as she walked out of the building. Two days later she got a call and was called in for an interview.

The interviewer was impressed with Marta's background and hired her "on the spot." The next training class will be in two days. The interviewer said, "We have a new trainer. He's tough but I hear he's good at what he does." Two days later, Marta went to the training class and saw the attractively dressed man that she saw at the gas station. He introduced himself and Marta immediately recognized him and shook his hand.

"Hello young lady. It's nice to meet you. My name is Vladimir and I am your new teacher.

Chapter 3
Glenda

Glenda lived in a large house that was surrounded by 40 areas in Connecticut. Her father was known for his work on Wall Street and did well in the Stock Market. Her mother was a member of the garden club, theater society, and studied opera, classical music, and piano.

She was the organist for her church that catered to the elite of society. Glenda was only allowed to be with people who were from higher levels of society and she learned early what was expected of her and who she was allowed to associate with.

Her mom would say, "It's all about image and what people think about you. Your dad and I have worked hard to maintain this image of wealth so we could provide a good life for you."

Glenda said, "But we never see dad because he is always working."

"Glenda," her mom said with a sound of sympathy in her voice, "that is the price of having the lifestyle we have. Someone has to work hard to provide for us and your dad is good at what he does."

Glenda walked away and turned on her theater-sized television and saw stories about the poor and hungry and what was happening in the "poorer neighborhoods."

"Who would people choose to live there when they could live the life she had and have maids to serve her food, and clean the house?" Glenda said. "Mom, I'm going for a walk," she asked. Her mom said, "That's nice dear. Don't go too far away.

"Yes mom."

Glenda walked outside, shut the door, and marveled at the garden area in her front yard and told the gardener that it looks like Versailles with the manicured lawns, fountains, and statues. There are roses, lilies, bluebonnets, and sunflowers growing around the property and I don't know how you keep up with all the work that has to be done.

"Now Glenda don't you worry your pretty little head about what I do. You just focus on your schoolwork and being good to your mom and dad."

"I will! I'll talk to you later."

"Bye Glenda!" The gardener went back to trimming the hedges and bushes. Glenda could only walk on trails close to her house because her parents were afraid she might get kidnapped and held for ransom.

The piano teacher named Mrs. Gwinbee lived close by and taught Glenda classical music after school.

"Now Glenda," her teacher advised, "I don't want to hear you play
Boogie-Woogie, rock songs, or head banging music. As far as I am concerned a young lady of your standing should play classical pieces and that is what I will teach you."

Glenda remembered what her mother would say, "a good man will like the classics so it is important that you learn how to play this type of music."

Glenda practiced for two hours every day and became a concert organist. Glenda's mother got her an audition with the director of the symphony and got an opportunity to play a concerto for the director.

"What beautiful melodies. You play the song like it is a piece of fine art. You must be my concert organist." Glenda thanked the director and told her mother that she got the job.

Her mother said, "Let me go and thank him personally." Her mother walked over to the director and handed him a large amount of cash.

Glenda watched her mom talk to the director and was shocked to hear her mother say, "This is just what we agreed on."

The director said, "indeed ma'am." Her mother walked towards Glenda and she stood near the curtain with a heart-broken spirit.

"I thought it was because he liked my music. He liked me because he would get paid extra." Glenda tried to gain her composure when her mom walked up to her.

"What's wrong dear?"

"Nothing is wrong mom. I am just very happy." "That's good dear. Let's go home." A taxi brought them home and Glenda and her mother walked inside to a warm and spacious front room. Glenda could hear her dad's voice and was glad that he was home.

When she walked into the room where her dad was she heard him talking to someone in a tender and passionate way. He called her Mindy and Glenda recognized that Mindy was dad's secretary. He said that he would meet with her later tonight and said some suggestive things that a young girl would not want to hear her dad say, especially to another woman.

Glenda felt sick to her stomach and realized that dad was having an affair. Suddenly everything made sense about dad's excuses and business trips. Glenda felt heartsick but knew there was nothing she could do to change the situation with her mom and dad.

She walked towards the kitchen, opened the refrigerator, got a snack, and sat down at the kitchen table. *I wonder if mom knows about this.* She held her head in her hands and wondered what she would do if dad broke up their "*happy home.*"

Glenda was not prepared for her life to change and hoped for the best. She spoke to her mother and asked what she and her dad were doing.

Her mother lowered her head and said, "We're fine Glenda. Your dad and I are just fine."

Glenda could tell her mom was not telling the truth and that she had been crying. Glenda said, "Good. I am glad you are doing well."

"I'll see you at dinner, Glenda. I have to get ready for my bridge club luncheon."

Glenda started to walk away and then walked back to her mother and said, "I love you mom."

"Well I love you too dear!"

Her mother hugged her and said, "Now run along a girl who is only young once."

Glenda went to her room and hugged her pillow.

Someday I will find someone to love me and he will be faithful and really love me. I am not going to live my mother's life. The stock market crash nearly destroyed her dad and Glenda's parents had to relocate to a less expensive area.

Glenda went off to college with a scholarship and became an accountant. She catered to the upper crust of society and was paid well. Her mother and father got a divorce and her dad paid several thousands in alimony. Her dad never recovered from all the money lost in a *"Ponzi type"* scheme but was too proud to admit he had made some bad choices.

Mom kept herself busy and ended up remarrying an attorney that helped take dad *"to the cleaners."* Glenda never went back home and was determined to have a normal life and make new friends that would be in her circle, not her mom's or dad's.

Chapter 4

"Katie, you are the only woman for me. I want you to help me raise my son. My children are no longer living with me. My wife was crazy and was on heavy antidepressants. In fact my wives were crazy. You are the only one my mother likes," Edward said.

"Edward, I like your mom but I was hoping if I had a son I would have him a little younger.

"Katie, don't be silly. We will have a child someday but this way we can focus on each other and our friends. My son is 20 years old and he needs someone to take care of him... Katie thought of the things she was doing at 20 years old.

She was going to college, playing tennis, working two jobs, and taking care of her brother and sister.

"Don't you think you are spoiling him Edward?"

"Not at all because when he was a little boy, his mom took him out of the country and turned out to be crazy. He needs a stable mother image."

"OK, if you say so. "

Edward started to be jealous of her friends, make acquaintances, and the people she met in her town and Katie could not understand why he was so controlling. She convinced herself that he loved her and was worried about her.

He started questioning what she was doing and was suspicious of her. During their courtship, Katie was not allowed to have her own friends or to visit them. Edward made fun of her when she went to church and told her that he wouldn't marry her if she became too *churchy.*

He hit her and banged her into walls, put her down, and then when she cried, Edward would get on his knees, apologize, and say, *he loved her.*

Katie believed that he was just angry or had a bad day and would forgive him. They got married and Katie noticed that he started changing. His mother and children came first in the relationship. If she gave her opinion and it was different than his he would threaten to break something or hurt her.

Katie lived in fear but tried to not upset her husband because she knew the consequences of such behavior. It was hard to determine what would set her husband off. It could be his son, his mother, Ricardo, and a number of other reasons but she got the blunt of it.

Katie wondered what she had done to make him want to hurt her and when she asked he would say, "Because you keep repeating yourself." Katie planned a romantic afternoon listening to soft romantic music, like Frank Sinatra, in the backyard. He didn't like the music and pulled her down by her hair and took her by the neck and started choking her on the concrete.

This was one of the many times he would grab her by the throat or make fun of her, or talk against her family, but she continually forgave him. He threatened to end her life more than once and Katie wondered if the next time he hurt her might be her final day on earth.

Edward brought a handsome seventeen-year-old to the house and introduced him to Katie. "Katie, this is Ricardo. I will make sure that he will look out for you and make sure you are protected."

"Ricardo, this is my wife, Katie."

"Hello, Ricardo. It is nice to meet you. Are you hungry? We have plenty of food." Ricardo said, "Yes, I'm starving. We are not fed much at the foster home."
"Did you bring anything to swim in? You can join us at the pool."

Edward said, "I have some spare swim trunks. I think my son's would fit you." Edward looked at Katie and said, "Ricardo will be staying with us for a while."
Katie welcomed Ricardo, told him where the food was, and said, "Come on and eat." Ricardo liked Katie from the start because she reminded him of his mother, whom he lost at a young age.

Ricardo said, "I have finally found a family that will love me and take care of me."

Ricardo became a part of the family, and Katie was like a mother to him. Katie felt close to Ricardo, and he became like a son to her. One morning, Katie walked into the kitchen with her eyes blackened and swollen. She was crying and had bruises on her arms. Ricardo asked, "What happened? Who hurt you?"

"It was Edward. He gets upset at me sometimes when I don't do or say what he wants. We're okay."

Ricardo said, "Katie, all you have to say is to make him stop, and that will be the last time Edward ever hurts you."

"Thank you, Ricardo, but everything will be alright. Edward is just in one of his moods. We will be fine."

Ricardo knew that Edward was getting more violent towards Katie but did not know what to do. This was his home, and his only option was going back to foster care or moving out. Ricardo said, "If you are sure that he is just in a mood, I won't say anything, but I better not see him beating you, or he is a dead man."

"Don't say anything to him, Ricardo. I'll be fine."

Chapter 5

Vladimir and Marta

Vladimir said, "Something tells me you are a rookie. You know, wet behind the ears."

If you are an officer there are going to be things you don't agree with that surprise, stun, and shock you but you have got to keep it together. Valamir was right about that.

She saw many surprises in training and learned how to defend herself, stand in defense mode, and be ready to defend no matter what directions hands or feet are swinging.

Marta practiced her kicks, punches, and jabs in front of a mirror. Vladimir took a special interest in Marta and stood next to her as she learned to shoot, look for suspicious objects, and build cases using previous information given. Marta was brought up in a home where she felt safe and there was a neighborhood watch program in the neighborhood.

Nothing prepared her for seeing drive-through shootings, traffic tickets, or citations, or having to work her "beat" in the middle of the night. Marta's eyes were open to the crime, lies, and deceit in her city.

She was disgusted when she saw her local politicians working with the crime bosses and realized that the police are called to protect but no one was defending the police in doing their job.

Vladimir and Marta became a team because she was the top student in the Academy. The murder of her son changed her and made her heart hard and cold.

"They will pay for their crimes. They all will pay."

Vladimir said that crimes can only be corrected through the judicial system and to never take the law into your own hands.

Two years later, Vladimir told Marta, "You are going to have to find a new partner. I am going to be working with the FBI. I have taught you everything I know and then some. It is getting to where the 'student is teaching the teacher'."

"You can't leave, Vladimir. I am finally getting used to you and your poor sense of humor."

"Very funny, Marta. You are really hilarious." Marta thought about what it would be like to join the FBI and applied for an open position on the force. Her interview went well, and she was hired for her first job.

She sat in the classroom with the other agents and noticed Vladimir sitting at one of the desks. "So, Vladimir, you thought you were getting rid of me, huh?"

"Marta, what are you doing here? Are you following me?" Marta said, "You can't break up a good team."
The head of the FBI stood in front of the classroom and showed pictures of the top assassins in the United States who were posing a "threat to the nation and needed to be stopped." The slide projector was turned on and the head of the FBI pulled down the projector screen and turned off the lights. The first picture is of a mob boss named Edward.

"I am showing his first picture that was known by the number of murders he had done. This is a picture of Ricardo. Ricardo will stop at nothing to follow orders from his boss. Your assignment, should you choose to accept it, is to either bring them to justice or to find a way to get rid of them so they can't commit any more crimes. I need a team that works well together and can stop these dangerous men and women. Tell me, ladies and gentlemen, do I have any volunteers?"

Marta looked at Vladimir and raised her hand. Vladimir smiled at Marta and said, *"Well, I guess we're it!"*

Chapter 6
Toxic Love

Toxic Love is like the taste on your tongue of a passionate kiss. The thrill of passion yet to be made. That is Toxic Love. It grips you. Envelops you. Until you are consumed with the flames of desire. Nothing else can satisfy but his toxic love.

He was sitting at the bar, cracking jokes with his friends; his eyes were blue. His face was almost angelic with a perfect nose and cheekbones. His body, well, that was more than a woman could believe. He had the body of Adonis or a Greek god.

She smiled to herself. What a catch he would be. How exciting he would be. Marta said to herself, "Good girls don't think like that."

She couldn't help noticing that he kept looking at her with those sexy eyes. She started blushing. She turned towards the bar, and he was glancing at her. He smiled with that incredibly sexy smile.

He looked like he was undressing her with his eyes. She blushed. "I hope he doesn't come over here," she said to herself. She drank her drink quickly. She needed to leave before he noticed she was looking. She started to get up and motioned with the waiter to pay her tab. He started walking towards her.

He got to her table and asked if she wanted something to drink. His eyes were sultry and alluring. She wanted to say, "No," but she said "Yes."

He said, "What will you have?" She said, "A Chardonnay."

He motioned with the waiter. "We'll have a Chardonnay for the lady, and I'll have a rum and coke."

"Very good, Sir," said the waiter. He sat down next to her. "Great," she said to herself.
She was getting nervous but excited at the same time. Her heart beat faster. "Would you like to dance?" he said.

Before she could say no, he took her by the hand and led her onto the dance floor. Her heart melted as he put his arms around her and held her close to him. She had not been touched for a long time. His touch was ecstasy and made her wonder what the night might bring.

They danced to a new song called "The Final Goodbye." As he held her close, he sang the song. It was as if the song had been written just for her. To Marta, this seemed a little corny and made up.

However, she enjoyed the moment. She deserved to be pampered and danced with. He sang, *"Dearest Sweetheart. I love you, yes, I do. You know, I will always care for you. But, I must go. I'm sure you know. Please don't cry. Just one more kiss, then it's our final goodbye. I knew when we met. I'd never regret it. One sunrise, one sunset with you. But my journey takes a path. Few ever go. So I must bid you adieu. Till that moment, think of a day. When we'll marry. And I'll take you away. Until then, let us dance. I'll hold you tight. One more kiss, and it's the final goodnight."* He twirled her around as he sang.

Suddenly, it felt like they were the only ones in the room. They were the only ones that mattered. The only thing that was important was this moment and this man dancing with her. He twirled her around again. He looked into her eyes. She leaned forward and followed his steps. He talked to her of the times in Colorado and the Midwest. How hard life had been. How he believed in God and John 3:16. He talked about working hard on the farm and taking care of the cows, horses, and chickens.

He talked about the storms that hit their area that almost destroyed the crops and how they survived and worked together as a family.

Marta said to herself, "Maybe he's okay. He protected his family during the winter storms. He believes in Jesus. He is an American. More than anything else, he likes me."

They danced to another slow song. He asked her about her life. She told him that she came from a town that never slept. Traffic never stopped. She was on a time clock, the minute she woke up to the time she went to sleep. Her life was hectic. She had deadlines and quotas to meet in her job. She made just enough to pay her bills. Her family was busy as well. She did not see them very much. When she did see them, they seemed to get along.

Ricardo listened intently to her every word. Marta liked that someone was listening even though he was a stranger. She dreamed of working beside him on the farm. Cooking meals and raising children. It would be a simple life for a happier time.

He led her back to the table. The drinks were sitting there. Ricardo said, "Let's toast to a new romance and a chance to begin again. No more storms or hard times for us. It will be 'all gravy' from now on. Good luck and smooth sailing."

Just then, the waiter interrupted the romantic moment by saying, "Excuse me, Sir, you have a call." Ricardo excused himself and asked her to wait for him. He walked out of the room. Marta watched him walk away. She smiled and picked up her glass. She started drinking her wine and listening to the music.

Ricardo walked to the desk and picked up the phone. "Hello, who is this?" said Ricardo.

"It's Lola! Edward has found me. Some of his thugs are scouting out my apartment complex. I am really scared and don't know what to do." Lola said, trembling.

Ricardo frowned and thought for a minute. "I'll go over there. I just have to say goodbye to someone. Where are you?"

"I'm at the pier in New Haven. I can't tell you the exact location. But I know you will find me. You always do."

Ricardo answered, "I will find you wherever you are. Don't worry. I've got this."

He hurriedly hung up the phone and then anxiously gazed down at it. Then he looked up and said, "Here it goes again. Why do these people keep calling me to help?"

The desk clerk nodded in agreement. He shook his head. He wondered what he was going to say to Marta. Then he asked himself why it mattered. He had just met her. She was just another woman, or was she? He felt drawn to her. He came back with a concerned look and said, "I have some important business to take care of. Can I call you?"

"I don't even know your name," she answered.

"My name is Ricardo Montero. What is your name?" "Marta Jones," she replied.

She reluctantly gave him her number. He kissed her on the cheek and said, "I'll call you. Wait for me."

He looked at her with those blue eyes, smiled, and left the bar. Marta mused, "I will never hear from him again."

Little did she know that Ricardo would become a part of her every thought, action, and dream. He would have a part in her life and future events. She did not realize that he lived a life of mystery and intrigue and that his life was dangerous. He dealt with dangerous people on a regular basis. All she knew was that this was a moment in time. Instead of caring for others, someone cared for her. He treated her like a princess.

She walked in the door, and her little dog Biscuit was waiting for her. She was so excited she jumped on the couch and then onto the arm of the chair. She tried to stand up tall.

Marta held her in her arms and snuggled her. "I'll let you out, Biscuit. Have you been a good girl?" Biscuit jumped off the couch and ran to the door. "There is nothing like a dachshund," said Marta.

She turned on the television. There was something about the man on the television that looked familiar. He was saving a woman from a burning building. Before she could get a second look, he faded into the shadows. She let Biscuit in and got ready for bed.

In the meantime, Ricardo was responding to the cry for help from a friend he cared about. He found the apartment complex on the north side of town, near the pier. Lola Murray had said, "Someone is trying to break in!"

Needing to be incognito, Ricardo had disguised himself with black clothing, a wig, and a hat. Even in that outfit, he was alluring and dashing. He went through the back alley, climbed the stairs, and searched for Lola. He smelled smoke coming from one of the apartment buildings. He put his jacket over his head and broke into the apartment. The fireman asked who he was.

Just at that moment, he disappeared into the shadows. "I know who did this," said Ricardo, "and he will pay!"

Newscasters were talking about the hero who rescued the woman. Ricardo knew that he was in danger if he was recognized. Ricardo knew it was Edward, his boss, who had set the fire. Lola was a threat to him, and he was trying to get rid of her. Lola had been an agent for 10 years for Edward.

Now she had become dispensable to him. He had his thugs break the windows and pour gasoline on the floor. Then he had them torch the draperies and rugs in the room. Lola was asleep. She smelled smoke. She shook her head. Someone must have left the stove on. She started opening her eyes and saw smoke coming from the bottom of the door. She tried to turn the doorknob and burned her hand. *Ouch! OMG! What is happening? Someone help me out of here.*

Ricardo got to the apartment complex just in time to see the building was in flames.

He screamed out for his friend. "Lola, where are you?" "I'm here! Ricardo help me!"

Ricardo rushed in without thinking of his own safety. He could hardly breathe with the smoke and flames. Rafters were starting to come down.

"Lola, where are you? Tell me where you are!" "I'm here," a faint voice cried.

Ricardo kicked open the door. He screamed out for his friend. "Lola! Where are you?"

"I'm here!" she answered faintly.

"Ricardo, help me!" Gasping and near exhaustion, Ricardo finally kicked open the door to the bedroom.

Chapter 7

Shielding himself from the flames, Ricardo entered the room where Lola was. She was lying in a corner, afraid and crying. Ricardo picked her up. At this time, the fireman was outside trying to stop the fire. Lola was lying on the floor.

She had been beaten up and had bruises on her face and body. Ricardo held Lola in his arms and helped her down the fire escape. Sobbing, Lola cried, "Ricardo! Why would he do this? Why is he trying to kill me?"

"I don't know," said Ricardo, "but I need to make sure you are safe."

The fireman told Ricardo that he had arrived at the apartment complex just in time to see that the building was in flames. Cameramen started driving up to the apartment complex. A news reporter and camera crew came out of the truck.
They looked around to find someone to talk to about the fire.

One of the men on the camera crew exclaimed, "Look, up towards the top of the building!"

They saw a man holding a woman. He was taking her down the fire escape. The smoke and fire were consuming the building. People were running out of the building. Louisa, the reporter, stood in front of the building.

She turned on the microphone and motioned for the camera crew to record her. "There are strange events on the Northside today. An arsonist set fire to an apartment complex. Fire crews are trying to stop the fire. A courageous man is saving a woman."

Suddenly, Louisa lost sight of the man. "Wait! Where did he go?" He disappeared before she could get a clear picture of him. She started asking questions of the people running out of the building.

One man said, "Everything I own was in that building. Now it is going up in smoke."

Louisa inquired, "Who is that man who is coming down the fire escape?" The man replied, "I don't know. Who are you talking about?"

Louisa tried to ask more questions. Ricardo ducked away and hoped no one would see him. He did not realize that he would be known as the man without a face. He was now a hero.

Marta lay in bed thinking about the romantic man she met. Would she ever see him? Was this just a dream? She dreamed about him singing to her. She remembered him talking about playing classical guitar. She couldn't wait to hear him play. Maybe they could play guitar together. He had the voice of an angel.
She hugged her pillow and smiled.

She started thinking, who was the man on television? She wondered if the man on the television was Ricardo. It couldn't be! He was not the kind of man to be running into burning buildings. She wanted to know more about him. Something inside her said that he was too good to be true. Biscuit snuggled up beside her.
She gave her a hug and held her close. She finally fell asleep. She dreamed of dancing to a Latin tango. Biscuit dreamed of steak bones and licked her lips.

Katie Valatshi walked into the kitchen and picked up the teapot. She poured some water into the teakettle. She put the teapot on the stove and turned up the heat. She started thinking about when she had first met Edward. She was taking a walk near the ocean. She loved to hear the sound of the water as it crashed against the rocks. She loved to watch the seagulls fly. She would walk barefoot and feel the sand under her feet.

The water was cool and refreshing. As she walked along, she saw some people playing beach volleyball. There was a man that caught her eye. He served the ball and hit it over the net. The people on the other side missed. He served the ball again and it was hit back over by the other team. The man that was serving set up the attack with his teammates, and they bounced it back and forth between them. Then, one of the teammates gave a grin and bounced it back to the one who was serving. He spiked the ball across the net. His teammates cheered and congratulated each other. The one who was serving spotted Katie.

Her eyes were fixed on him. He walked over to her. He started walking with her on the beach. He asked her name and invited her to get together for drinks at the Ocean Cove Bar. She went with him. He was the life of the party. Everybody liked him. She noticed his concern for his friends and their families. How he would talk about caring for his mother and his son. He believed in the teachings of John 3:16. They got married, and

Katie noticed that he started changing. His mother and children came first in the relationship. If she gave her opinion and it was different than his, he would threaten to break something or hurt her. Katie lived in fear but tried not to upset her husband because she knew the consequences of such behavior. It was hard to determine what would set her husband off. It could be his son, his mother, Ricardo, and a number of other reasons, but she got the brunt of it. Katie wondered what she had done to make him want to hurt her, and when she asked, she was told it was because she kept repeating herself.

Edward went into the study and made a call. He picked up the phone and dialed a number.

When asked why he was doing this, he would say, "Because you keep repeating yourself."

Katie planned a romantic afternoon listening to soft romantic music, like Frank Sinatra, in the backyard. Edward didn't like the music and pulled her down by her hair and took her by the neck and started choking her on the concrete. This was one of the many times he would grab her by the throat and look deep into her eyes. Katie couldn't breathe.

She heard footsteps and was afraid Edward would see her cry. She tried to wipe her tears. She pretended to start reading so he wouldn't hurt her. Katie started packing a suitcase. "What the hell are you doing?" Edward violently ripped the suitcase in half and threw it across the room. She tried to run out the door. He grabbed her by the hair, threw her down, and started choking her. She begged to leave.

Her husband told her to go to her room. Katie started crying and begged to leave. Leonardo, Edward's son, demanded, "Go to your room."

She tried to run out the garage, but he knocked her down. She started crying, and he told Leonardo that she fell and tripped.

He told his son, "Look at her. Look at her lying there."

They both stared at her in contempt. She finally got out of the garage, but he found her. Glaring at her, Edward declared, "No one will believe you, Katie. They will think you are crazy. You're an idiot. Everyone knows what a nice guy I am. Look how good I am to my mother! Who will believe you?"

Katie went inside. Edward walked over to her, like he was a different person. He gently asked, "Please forgive me. When you go on and on I get angry. You know I love you."

Katie was crying. She wanted to believe him. He took her to their bed and made passionate love to her. She started trying to trust him again. Until the next time he would turn on her, she would stay. Surely, he would not hurt her again. Katie knew this happened so often and that it would not change. She thought, "*If I love him enough, if I don't repeat myself, maybe he will love me. Maybe he won't hurt me.*"

Chapter 8

Marta Jones woke up to her normal routine. The alarm went off. Biscuit had to relieve herself and go outside. She had just enough time for coffee, her morning jog, and devotionals. As she was drinking her coffee, the phone rang. Could it be him? No. He wouldn't call her. That was just a shot in the dark. It would be a chance encounter.

The phone declared, "He is like an angel tearing through the night to rescue the weak and the weary."

The reporter said, "More news at 5:00 as the news crew investigates the fire and the brave hero who saved the day."

By the time she had jogged 3 miles, she headed home to get ready for work. She was still thinking of the story. Who was this mysterious man? Could it be him? Could this be the reason he had to go away? Should she ask him at the Bistro tonight?

She went to work, and the day went by. She told herself, "He probably won't show up. This was too unreal to be believed."

Yet, out of curiosity and nothing else to do, she went to the Bistro. She had made an attempt to fix her hair and makeup. She was wearing a pretty dress that had been in the closet for 6 months. She wore black pumps to look taller.

She walked in, and he was sitting at a table, waiting for her. She smiled and tried to be cordial. She felt like a schoolgirl. He got up from his seat, walked over to her, and gave her a kiss. He took her by the hand and led her to the table he had reserved just for them.

Maria, the owner at the Bistro, started singing "Take a Chance." It had a haunting, jazzy melody.

Ricardo asked her to dance, and once again held her in his arms. Maria sang, *"A new breeze is blowing. Something is showing. There is a wind of change in the air. You feel him entreating. Your heart is repeating a love song where lyrics fill the air. You smile, and you say, it might be ok, to trust and believe once again. But trust is a word that's no longer heard.*

Your heart can't be broken again. I'm the one you've waited to see. You don't have to struggle again. Let's take this dance; let's start this romance. For now we will be more than friends. Come dance to the music. I'll play a slow song. It's time for our love to begin. I'm the one you've been waiting to see. You don't have to be lonely again."

After the song, Ricardo led her back to the table by the window. There was a lovely view of the ocean. There was music from the 50s and 60s playing in the background. It felt like someone had turned back the clock to a bygone era.

He ordered her favorite wine. "Marta, I feel like I've known you all my life." "How is that? You hardly know me."
"I know your heart," said Ricardo.

"You inspired me, Marta, with your beautiful guitar playing."

He opened his guitar case. He picked up his guitar out of the case. He started tuning the keys. There was an old song playing, called "Besame Mucho." He started playing the Spanish guitar and singing to her. His eyes were like blue pools. His face was fair. His hair glowed in the candlelight. His mouth sang such passionate words. He played the guitar like it was his lover.

She was lost in the music. She closed her eyes and pretended she was in Spain in a town so long ago. He implored, "Sing with me, Marta."

Marta started singing the song in Spanish. Ricardo harmonized with her. He sang some other songs to her and then asked her to play. She played some of the songs that she played during Open Mic sessions. Ricardo listened to her. He found another guitar and started playing music with her. They were able to blend and make sweet harmony in their music. They sang for what seemed like hours. She was lost in the music. He could only see the passion she inspired in him.

Ricardo asked if she wanted a glass of wine. She tried to compose herself and have normal conversation. "So, Ricardo," she began, "What brought you to town?"

Ricardo suddenly got quiet. "There are dark forces here you don't understand. There are those who must crusade against them. That way others can sleep at night."

"What do you mean?" asked Marta.

He looked at her and smiled. "This is not the time for sadness but a time for us."

Marta was puzzled. What was he talking about? What was he called to do? The rain started coming down outside and lightning struck the building. The lights started to flicker and went dim. Ricardo saw a figure coming towards them with eyes as dark as night. He was carrying a sword. Menacingly, the figure shouted, "I told you, Marta, what would happen if I saw you with another man!"

He started coming towards Marta. There was fire in his eyes. Ricardo recognized him and exclaimed, "Vladimir!"

Acting quickly, Ricardo exclaimed, "Step behind me, Marta. I will stop him!"

Ricardo retrieved the sword hidden beneath his chair and challenged Vladimir Muriat to a duel. They crossed swords and fought a fierce battle. Ricardo raised his hands in a circle around them. They spun in a circle till they were both gone. Ricardo came back alone. The lights turned back on, and everyone wondered what had happened. Marta had not realized that she was one of the few to see the warrior from the mist.

Ricardo said, "We must go. It is not safe here. I will drive you home."

Puzzled and dazed after the scene she had just witnessed, Marta inquired, "Will someone explain to me what is going on?"

"You will see soon enough," reassured Ricardo.

"Just know I am here to protect you." He drove her home, and she invited him in for hot chocolate and to listen to music.

As she was making the hot chocolate, he turned the radio to a jazz station. She brought the hot chocolates into the living room. He started a fire in the fireplace. The sound of the cracking fire, BB King in the background, and warm hot chocolate was heaven to Marta. He snuggled close to her on the couch. He put his arms around her and gave her a passionate kiss. She snuggled close to him. They fell asleep as BB King played on.

She woke up in the middle of the night and realized she was half-dressed and lying beside Ricardo. He held her so gently and tenderly. He looked into her eyes and gave her another passionate kiss. She went back to sleep in his arms.

Meanwhile, Vladimir Muriat was very angry. What a cheap show trick! How did I end up outside the restaurant?

Ricardo had stopped him from getting Marta. Marta had been his love for years. He just wasn't the marrying kind. He sang, to the sound of the conga drums, a song of vengeance. "*I am a warrior. I stand tall and true. I am a warrior. I am as good as you. I am a warrior. If I should die in this place another will rise and you will see my face. Some have tried to stop me in the race. I kept on going, so I would win the race. I am a warrior. I dance to a different tune. I will ride on, till I see the rising moon. So go your way, and I will go mine too. I'm a warrior. I've fought tougher men than you. Goodbye to things, I've left behind. I will find a land that I can claim as mine. I am a warrior! Warrior!*"

Angrily, Vladimir said to himself, "Ricardo, you don't know who you are messing with. But I know who you are, and soon Marta will know too!"

He headed back to his home, showered, and went to work.

When Marta woke up, he was gone. She started coffee. Then she realized something! Her car was still at the bistro! She asked herself what she should do now. She looked outside, and there was her car. Did she just dream of him? Was this just some sick fantasy of a love-starved woman? She closed the door. "He's not real!" She prepared to go to work. As she opened the car door, she saw a note with a rose on the visor. The note said, "Till next time."

Ricardo drove towards the airport and caught his flight. He had to go to his homeland and wait for instructions. He didn't want Marta to know, but he was from a country full of poverty, filth, and crime. It was where people begged for food and cold water to drink. This is where the good becomes bad in one easy lesson. The wise are always ready, so there are no surprises. He was wise and up to the challenge.

Chapter 9

The big boss came over and told him about a job he was expected to do. All Ricardo could think of was her brown eyes and the way she looked in the candlelight.

He was supposed to pick up a box and bring it to Hurley's Park. He had to do his job. He was told that what he was expected to get was in a safe deposit box at the bank. He was supposed to tell them he was Mr. Goodman, and there would be no question. Ricardo did as he was instructed. He got the box and took it with him. He drove to Hurley's Park where there was a cemetery. He shuddered at the thought of even going near that place. He was instructed to leave the box in the cemetery. The box had a smell of mold, mildew, and burning flesh.

He opened up the gate, and the hinges were old and squeaky. He was suddenly afraid although he was not sure of what. He gathered up his courage and walked in.

He felt like someone was joining him in the walk. He laid the box down next to a gravesite, and he could hear a voice calling his name. It was soft and sweet. It sounded familiar. Like someone he had known before. He walked back towards the gate and felt a cold hand on his shoulder. His blood curdled, and he did not dare look at who he didn't know how long Marcus will be able to keep you here.

You need to give thought about what you want to do. You are a good marksman, and you were a top agent. There has to be a calling for that.

Nodding in agreement, Lola answered, "Ricardo, this is all I know."
"I can totally relate," answered Ricardo.
"Right now, I have to catch a flight and head back to find out what my next assignment will be."

"Did you even ask what was in that box you brought to the cemetery?" Lola asked.

Ricardo answered, "No, I don't question the boss. It's not healthy."

Ricardo once again shuddered when he thought about what would be inside the box. Lola smiled. "I would have asked. I would not have cared what he thought."

Ricardo replied, "That's why you're here, Lola."

Lola cringed. "Your turn is coming, Ricardo. Say or do the wrong thing, and you'll be running too."

"Hopefully, that won't happen," answered Ricardo.

They drove up to the hideout and stopped the car. Marcus heard them drive up and walked towards the car. Ricardo introduced Lola to him. Ricardo thanked Marcus. He gave Lola a hug and said goodbye. He walked to his car. He put the keys in the ignition and started thinking what Lola had said. Dismissing the thought, he declared that it would never happen to him.

He drove through the woods and headed towards the airport. After arriving, he drove into the airport parking, parked his car, and then walked towards the ticket counter and got his tickets. He went through the line to have them check his baggage and personal things.

He walked towards the coffee shop as he waited for his flight. He thought to himself that the boss had another assignment for him. He said that this one would be easier. Ricardo hated this job. He hated his boss and what he had to do to earn a living. Life isn't fair when you are coming from my side of the streets. The flight would lead him to the boss's villa. He got on board the plane, buckled his seatbelt, and waited for the plane to take off.

The boss had told him, "I'll meet you for lunch, and we will discuss the details." The plane landed. Ricardo walked out of the plane and headed to the rental car check-in where he discovered that a rental car had been reserved for him. The boss had a hotel reserved for him also.

He drove to the hotel, checked in, and then opened the door to his room. He noticed that the hotel room had a few pictures on the walls but not much to see. However, it had some modern conveniences. It had a refrigerator, microwave, and a television. He put his bags on the bed. He took a shower and freshened up.

He was told to meet the boss at 2:00 p.m. at his home. What the boss had to talk to Ricardo about was not for the public. He got in his car and headed to his boss's villa. It was like a castle compared to what he had lived in. He drove into a parking place and parked the car.

He knocked on the door. "Who is it?"

"It is Ricardo." "Come in. He is expecting you."

Ricardo walked in. There was a chandelier on the ceiling. He recognized paintings from artists like Van Gogh, Monet, and Rembrandt. Flowers were sitting on antique cabinets, and mirrors lined the walls. The floors were oak. There was a cherry wood table with fresh fruit, nuts, and candy trays on it and a hallway leading to the stairs.

The boss said, "Come in, Ricardo. Mi casa es su casa! Take off your shoes and relax. What do you want to drink?"

Ricardo answered, "I'll have a rum and coke."

The boss served rum and coke to Ricardo. Pouring himself a gin and tonic, the boss smoothly inquired, "Ricardo, how long have we been working together?"

"Since you picked me off the streets as an orphan," Ricardo replied.

Nodding in agreement, the boss continued, "Ricardo, I plan to make you a very rich man. You will have everything you have dreamed of. You will have fancy cars, money, a beautiful wife, and retirement. Sounds good? What I am going to be asking you is easy money. Are you interested?"

Ricardo replied, "What are you asking me to do?"

The boss evaded the question by saying, "Not yet. I'll tell you after lunch. Lunch is ready."

The lunch was in the formal dining area. The meal consisted of a mixed salad with soup, fresh rolls, and sliced cheeses. For the entrée, he had chicken with rice and vegetables. It was the best meal he had had in a long time. For dessert, there was a dark chocolate cake with cherries and whipped cream on top. It had been divided into sections with raspberries and strawberries mixed with cream cheese and whipped cream between the layers. It was so good that he had to have another slice. One of his servants poured coffee for him and the boss. He motioned for her to leave the room.

After lunch, the boss talked freely to Ricardo about his assignment. "Now I want to talk to you about what I have called you here to do. I want you to get access to internet banking codes. It will take some charm, pizazz, and a good con job.
Surely you can get someone to feel sorry for you and send money. What do you think?"

Ricardo noticed the boss's computer and got an idea. "I could use internet dating sites. No one gets physically hurt. They think they are doing it for a good cause. They want to give their money away."

"Brilliant!" exclaimed the boss.

"Tell me how much money you need, and I will make it happen."

Ricardo replied, "I will need to change my face and hair. I will call myself William Monroe. Can you have a mask made that I can put on to disguise my looks?"

The boss replied, "I will have our makeup artist make some changes in your appearance. You will look 20 years younger when she is done with you!"

Ricardo laughed. "Let me think? How old would that make me? Don't make me look too young. I want the older ones to think they still have a chance!"

They both laughed. After checking his calendar, the boss stated, "All right. I will have Linda fix you up tomorrow. Come to her shop at 10 a.m."

The boss handed Ricardo his card. "You keep up the good work, Ricardo. You are destined for a high position with me."

"Thanks," Ricardo replied. "You have been a good boss. You've taken good care of me."

The boss replied, "I take care of those who care for me and the business."

Invitingly, the boss asked, "Come and join me at the pool. I have some extra swim shorts you can wear."

After thanking his boss, Ricardo went to the bathroom, pulled off his clothes, and changed into the swim trunks. He couldn't help thinking about what Lola said.
He hoped she was all right. He hoped that the boss did not suspect he had helped her. The boss was sitting in a lounge chair by the pool. He had two beautifully tanned women by his side.

The boss noticed him looking. "Either one could be yours. You just name which you want."

They both looked at him. He quickly answered, "They're not my type. I don't have any trouble getting dates."

"Suit yourself, Ricardo. You tell me what you want, and it's yours."

Ricardo dived into the lukewarm water in the pool, swam towards the bottom, and came up for air.

He swam some laps and relaxed by the side of the pool. "Care to join me in the Jacuzzi?" his boss asked.

The boss and his two women got in. Ricardo joined them. The water was hot. The waiter started some jazz music and served cool drinks. Ricardo relaxed in the Jacuzzi for another half hour.

Tiredly, Ricardo asked, "Boss, I need to go to the hotel and get some rest." "Don't forget your appointment," the boss reminded him.

"Can't wait to see what she comes up with."

"Neither," said Ricardo in a hesitant voice. "Hopefully, it won't be permanent."

The boss laughed. "Just permanent enough for the game we're playing." Ricardo went into the bathroom, changed out of his swimwear, and put on his clothes.

He headed towards the door. "Ricardo, I am counting on you. You are one of my best workers."

Reassuringly, Ricardo answered, "I won't let you down, boss." "Good!"
He said goodbye to the boss and headed out the door. He opened the car, put the keys in the ignition, and drove away. He got back to the hotel late. He walked in, set the alarm, and fell asleep. He dreamed of dancing with Marta.

He remembered the time he had met her aunt at the villa. She had been sitting by herself and listening to live music. He asked if he could join her. Her name was Marie Van Scente. She told him what a charming young man he was. She talked about her niece, who was living in town and going to college.

"She needs a nice young man like you. She is going to inherit my wealth if anything happens to me. She has been a wonderful niece. I would love to introduce you two."

Marie showed him a picture. Ricardo remembered saying that she was beautiful. "Yes, and she is innocent from so much of the world. She is going to college and staying in a dorm. I will be visiting her soon."

Ricardo listened and made a mental note regarding Marta. He planned to meet her. Who would have expected that a chance encounter at a bar would bring her into his life?

Chapter 10
Day of the Wolf

Edward Muriat was Ricardo's boss. He closed the door and called for his wife Katie. Katie was lying on the bed. She could hear his footsteps.

She was afraid to get up. Edward turned the mattress over on her and said, "Get up! Didn't I tell you to get up? You better apologize to me before I get home, or you will get worse!"

Katie got up, stood in the corner, and trembled with fear. He told her to come over to him. She did as she was told and apologized as he told her to do.

"You make me so angry, Katie. You go on and on. You make me this way." "I'm sorry, Edward. If you don't want me, I will leave."

Edward said, "I will just tell people you had sex with someone else and that I had to get rid of you. I'm going to work." His mother called, and he had a friendly, loving conversation with her. Katie was glad for the relief. She prayed again, God please help me. Help me find a way out.

Katie got the brunt of his wrath. She would say yes, dear. Whatever you say, dear. But she was beginning to despise the man she married. He was evil, corrupt, and vain.

"Katie! You need to hope and pray that Ricardo does what he is told. You know what happens if someone does not do what I say?" asked Edward.

"Yes, I do," Katie said, trembling with fear. "Is there anything you need, dear?" Katie was shaking. This was not the first time she heard his threats. He had a reputation of getting rid of people who bored him or knew too much. He walked swiftly towards her and grabbed her arm. Do you want this arm, Katie? Don't disobey me!"

"Please don't hurt me, Edward. I'll be good. I will do what you say."

Angrily, Edward ordered, "Go clean something unless you want me to break something of yours!"

Shaking, Katie pleaded, "Please don't. I'll stay out of your way. Just don't hurt me."

Edward laughed. "You are lucky I am in a good mood, Katie." She left the room and started crying. She prayed to God, "Please help me to find a way of escape. I am so frightened of him." She wept as she cleaned the kitchen.

Edward went back to the Jacuzzi and smiled at his good fortune. Edward was gone all night. Katie was glad that he was gone. He was not able to hurt her.

When Katie met Edward, he seemed so sweet and charming. He wined and dined her. She had inherited money from her family and was living well. Edward seemed like he loved her. She married him without hesitation.

Once they were married, he made sure his name was on her accounts. He embezzled funds, started making fun of her, and stopped all her friends from being in her life.

Then, she became his "trophy wife" and was his "rich woman." She started seeing his angry side. She asked about visiting her friends. He took her by the hair, threw her down, and started choking her.

"You are not going anywhere unless I tell you can go," Edward would say.

She was very frightened. She couldn't breathe. He finally let her go. She went to the bedroom and started crying. She noticed the bruises on her neck. She asked herself, what had she gotten into? From that point on, she tried not to upset him. She "walked on eggshells" so she wouldn't make him mad. She never knew what would set him off.

At Ricardo's hotel, the alarm went off and he got up. Ricardo looked at himself in the mirror and realized that he would look different in the photo. I wonder what I am going to look like. Maybe they can make me look 20 years younger.

Hmmm…. He got in the shower and enjoyed the warm water as he bathed.

He toweled off, got dressed, and found a place to eat. The time change was getting to him. He had to get used to the change in time. He drank some coffee and thought about Marta. What would she think if she knew what he did? Could they ever have a normal life? She was the type of woman he had always dreamed of. Someday she will be mine. Maybe once I do this job, I can give Marta the kind of life she deserves. She will never have to work again.

He arrived at the makeup artist's room on time. She told him to sit down in the chair. She showed him pictures of movie stars, artists, and rock stars. Who do you want to look like? He pointed to a picture of an actor from the silver screen. That is a perfect choice. You already have a profile for him. I just have to make some minor adjustments. She performed her makeup artistry. This took two hours of making the mask and adding touches to make it realistic. She put it on him. He looked in the mirror and did not recognize himself. He took a second look and smiled. You did it!

She had some casual clothes laid out for him. He excused himself and changed in one of the rooms. When he came out, he was William Monroe. He looked like a college student looking for a date. He looked up dating sites on his laptop. He spotted one that was too far out to be believed. It was called "I'm into you."

He straightened his clothes and gave a casual smile. He took his picture and completed the dating profile. He waited to see who would be his first target. The one he least expected, yet wanted to see, was on the site. It was Marta. He didn't want her to know what he was doing.

He started getting messages from women on the site. "They all want a piece of me," he surmised.

He devised a plan on how to get them to send money. It would be for a charitable cause. Something they could feel good about. He wrote more on his profile about helping lost souls. He had the hook and the bait.

On his profile, he wrote: "Come follow me. Come follow me to a land that's beautiful and bright. You will be my delight every night. Come follow and believe again. Don't you believe there is a chance for romance and that love is leading you? Come follow me."

Glenda Smith took the bait. His cause seemed so meaningful and good. He seemed genuine. His site showed pictures of people doing charitable things. She believed in saving the planet. She could spare $50.00 here or $100.00 there, as long as she budgeted for it.

She wrote to William Monroe (Ricardo's alias), "I will help you! I care about the people you are helping."

"Oh, my love," he said.

"Wait till I meet you. I will make you a happy woman. Then I will take care of you."

Glenda had been lonely. Meeting someone like William was a dream come true. Ricardo laughed. She bought it! I can't believe anyone would be so trusting! He started getting messages from other women. They winked and wanted to meet him. This is too easy, thought Ricardo.

He told them where to send the money. He knew a courier who could get the money to him. They gladly agreed to help. He would tell the ladies how desperate he was. He told them that he had been listening to them. He talked about his love for them.

He also told them how telling his boss that he would not ask for money got him in trouble and that he couldn't leave Nigeria now unless they sent him more money. He even convinced them that they had to open new bank accounts for him. Ricardo could not believe they would do this. However, they did everything he asked.

Leslie Ronaway was another victim of Ricardo's. She was in her 50's and had lost the love of her life. Ricardo seemed like someone she could trust. He asked her for money to help him out of a "dangerous situation."

She sent him money with no reservations. Her husband had just been laid to rest. However, his ghost watched her as she wrote to Ricardo. He tried to tell her to stop. She was being deceived. Leslie could not hear him. He tried to whisper in her ear that William Monroe was evil. Leslie still could not hear him. Leslie just rubbed her ear. She got up from the computer, shut it off, and walked towards the door. Like a robot, she opened the door, walked to the car, and opened the door of the car.

She put the keys in the ignition and then looked in the visor mirror. Thinking she saw her husband's face, she trembled and laid her head down on the steering wheel. I have to find happiness again. I am so lonely. She went to the customer service area of her local Walmart and filled out a form to send money.

Even though she was warned by the customer service lady not to send money, she lied and said she knew to whom she was sending it. She finished the transaction and was assured that the money she sent to him should arrive in an hour.

Ricardo called his boss. "Ricardo! How did it go?" asked Edward. "Easy money!" answered Ricardo.

"You would not believe how easy it is!" The boss shook his head. "How trusting! How gullible!" The boss laughed.

"Are you still trying to win Marta's affection?"

"Yeah, but she sees right through me. She is not buying it."

The boss answered, "You know, she will inherit billions in property and land."

"I know," Ricardo agreed, "but there is something about her. She has a gift of perception into people."

"Dazzle her! Make her believe you!" the boss suggested.

Ricardo replied, "I'll keep trying. But she's not as trusting as Glenda." Ricardo wryly remembered that he had stated he was from the Dakotas in his profile. Ricardo knew he had never been to the Dakotas in his life. He took off the mask and changed his clothes.

Later, he drove back to the motel, checked out, and then caught a flight back to Marta's town. After paying the parking fee, he got into town just in time to hear Marta's last set.

Chapter 11

Marta was performing on stage at a local theater. She had the crowds cheering with her guitar and melodic voice as she sang a Guns and Roses song. She sang it like it was her own. Suddenly, she saw Ricardo coming into the door and made a sound as if in shock.

Then she proclaimed to her audience, "I am performing a new song for the first time. It is a song of love and passion." She strummed on the guitar and played a haunting melody.

Then she sang, "*How I long for his love. Oh my love, how I long for your touch. How I long to feel what real love is like. He leads a double life, but I'm still his wife. He says it's for me. He fights for liberty. When he goes away, I say, just one more day. Let him come safely home to me. I may never know the path he goes. He says it's for me to protect our family. When he flies away, I say, just one more day. Let him come safely home to me.*
How I long for his love. How I long for his touch. Oh my love, how I long to feel what real love is like."

Ricardo was mesmerized. The crowd was quiet for a few minutes. Then they stood up in thunderous applause. She bowed, and the curtain closed. Ricardo smiled and clapped for her.

Marta whispered under her breath, "Oh my. I wonder what theatrics he will do this time. He is not real. This is all for show. I can't believe him."

She looked at Ricardo as he stood amidst the crowd. She smiled. She opened up the curtain and took another bow to the audience. It was the final curtain call.

She went backstage to help with the band equipment. Ricardo was waiting for her. "You were magnificent!" "Thank you," she graciously replied.

"When did you get here?" Ricardo asked.

"Oh, I've been here for a while," Marta answered.

Ricardo invited her out to dinner. He was charming as always. Marta looked in his eyes. "What is your game? Who are you?"

She looked at him with such clarity that he almost wanted to tell her the truth. "Who do you think I am? I'm Ricardo! I told you that!"

"That's not what I mean. You are too smooth. You are too perfect." "Can't a man show you a good time without your being suspicious?" "Yes," said Marta.

"You just don't believe someone could love you. That's your problem." "Ricardo, tell me about your family." He got a very serious look on his face. "I can't tell you about them. The less you know about me, the better." "Why?"

"It's for your safety. If you knew more about me you would be in danger. Just trust me, ok?"

Marta replied, "I will trust you for now." Ricardo asked, "So, Marta, how was your day?" "I worked," said Marta.

"It was a hard day. How was your day?" "Bad day here too," said Ricardo.

"Believe me, you don't want to know."

They toasted with a glass of wine. "Marta, I have to tell you. I am falling for you. Could you take a chance on me?"

Marta was surprised. He walked over to her side, sat down, put his arms around her, and gave her a passionate kiss. She looked in his eyes and kissed him back. "How about it, Marta? Will you be mine?"

"I don't know." Just as she said that, he gave her another passionate kiss. She felt dizzy.

He kissed her again. "It's the candlelight and the wine. I almost believe you."

Marta told him about the music she was working on and the audience. She was hoping to get into music in a big way. She could get out of her clerical job and do what she loved. "I could make that happen," said Ricardo.

"Whatever you want Marta... I just want to make you happy and love you." In the meantime, Glenda was starting to wire money, per Western Union, to William Monroe (alias Ricardo). She was still hopeful that she and Bill would end up together. She was hopeful that all the things he promised her would come true. He had given her the name to wire the money to as well as the state and the code.

William Monroe had promised that he would take her away to a life of adventure. He would introduce her to his family. She believed every word. The more she sent, the more he promised. She told herself that she would do this for love. She would do this to please William. However, she started noticing amounts of money were being transferred over the internet that she did not authorize. Glenda Smith knew she had not made them.

She started being suspicious. Could these withdrawals and debits be from him? Had he found access to her banking information? She had to find out. Little did she know she was just one of the many women he was scamming over the internet? She thought she was the only one. Marta went home and took care of Biscuit. She lay in bed thinking about Ricardo. Could she trust him? Who was he really? What was she going to do about Vladimir? She started reading a mystery story. She felt tired, got ready for bed, and fell asleep.

When she woke up, she started the coffee and began to get ready for work. As she was leaving, the rain started pouring down. The weather report predicted flash floods. She merged onto the interstate. A car from another lane started speeding and almost hit her. She started skidding. Luckily, she did not hit anybody. She got off her exit and drove towards her building. She walked in and poured herself a cup of tea. She headed towards her desk. As usual, there was a mountain of paperwork waiting for her.

At lunch, she met with an old friend, and they shared love and losses. Marta couldn't wait to tell her about Ricardo. "Watch out for him," said her friend Brenda.

"I know his type."

"Don't worry. I'm watching him," Marta reassured her.

She went back to work and noticed someone was watching her from the parking lot. It looked like Vladimir, but she couldn't be sure. She went inside and attempted to get more work done.

As she opened the door, there was Ricardo. Ricardo declared, "You know all that I want is you."

"Ricardo, I did not expect to see you."

"I wanted to make sure you were all right with the storm. Can I come in?" "Yes," replied Marta.

"Take off your raincoat. Would you like a glass of wine or some coffee?"

Putting his coat on the chair, Ricardo answered, "I'll take a glass of wine." Biscuit started snarling and barking at Ricardo. "I don't get it. Dogs normally like me."

"It's ok, Biscuit. He won't hurt us." Biscuit barked, gave him a look, and walked away. They talked until the lights turned on.

"You better go. I have to work tomorrow. I'll talk to you tomorrow." He gave her another passionate kiss. It's getting harder to leave you, Marta. I am looking forward to when I don't leave you at all."

Forcefully, Marta answered, "I need to work tomorrow. Goodnight, Ricardo."

She got ready for bed and noticed Ricardo was still in the yard. Why doesn't he leave? She locked the doors and windows. She lay in bed and noticed Ricardo was still in the yard. She asked herself, that doesn't make sense he's still here.

What is he doing? She lay in her bed dreaming about Ricardo. She wondered why he followed her. What was he thinking? She heard a thud in the basement. She had no reason to believe someone was downstairs. She heard a crash. Did she dare look?

Chapter 12

She put on her robe and headed down to the basement with a baseball bat, which was the first weapon she found. She hears some and then gets rid of his victims before they discover who he really is.

"Who is he really?" asked Glenda.

"He has been playing people for years. He is the man without a face. He is like a shadow. You don't notice him until its too late. He is not someone you want to get mixed up with."

Worriedly, Glenda cried, "What will I do?"

"Wait to do anything till you hear from me. Don't let him know you are on to him," warned Vladimir.

"I will try," promised Glenda.

I just can't believe he would deceive me like this." Vladimir looked at her.

"You know, Glenda. You're not a bad looking girl. In fact, you are very pretty. You don't need to beg someone to love you."

"Thanks, Vladimir, but that doesn't help me now."

"Maybe it won't help you," Vladimir answered, "but don't settle if you don't have to."

Glenda said goodbye to Vladimir and went home. She lay on her bed and cried herself to sleep. When she thought of how she was taken, she hit the pillow and cried more. She lay down and wondered what Vladimir would have her do.

Ricardo asked Marta if he could play her guitar. Marta was surprised. She didn't even know he could play. Ricardo said, "I wrote you a song about how I feel about you. Would you like to hear it?"

Marta said, "Sure!" She said this more out of curiosity than caring. He held the guitar like a baby and played a beautiful melody.

"You don't believe you could be loved, but I do. That someone would climb the highest mountain, just for you. That I would swim the seven seas. That they would bow on their knees. Just to love only you, but I do. You've been hurt before, but I'm here to offer more. We can find a love that can be sweeter for you and me. If you will just give me half a chance, we can start a new romance. We'll have a life of love and happiness. I've loved before. My heart's been broken and torn. I didn't think I could love again till I met you. I knew you would be true. My heart's now on the mend." Ricardo played with such passion and technique that she was amazed in watching him play. He was an accomplished classical guitar player.

"Marta, I know you don't believe in someone who loves you. I know I have used that word before and not really meant it. But Marta, believe that I mean it when I say it to you." He laid down the guitar and gave her a kiss.

He massaged her back and held her close to him. She was caught up in the moment. She held him close as he embraced her. She felt the passion come back into her heart that she thought was lost. She surrendered herself to the moment as he kissed her again.

The next day, he made a decision that he would tell Marta everything and that he would no longer deceive her. He decided to talk to his boss about Marta and to tell him to leave her alone.

He called his boss and told him that he wanted to meet with him. "Sure, Ricardo. What do you want to talk about?"

Ricardo answered, "I'd rather tell you in person. Let's meet at the diner." "Ok, but what's wrong?" his boss asked.

Ricardo answered, "As I said, I'd rather tell you in person." "Ok. You know you are like a son to me, Ricardo. I'll meet you."
They met at the diner, and the boss had his men with him. "Hello, Ricardo! I see business is going well! Money is rolling in!"

"Boss," Ricardo began, "there is something I want to tell you. I don't want to do this anymore."

"Do what?" the boss asked.

"Deceive Marta," Ricardo answered. "I love her, and I don't want her hurt. I don't want anyone but her."

"So you don't want a paycheck anymore? Well, I bet there are plenty that do!" "I want to work with you, but I just don't want to hurt Marta."
"You know, in our business, it's hard to keep a wife, but there are plenty of women out there."

"I know," Ricardo responded, "but there is only one for me."

"Tell you what. As long as you continue to bring money in through the dating site, you can have whomever you want. However, I am warning you, Ricardo. If you betray or cross me, there will be consequences."

"I know," answered Ricardo.

"I've seen your consequences." The boss gave him a hug and raised his glass. "To you and Marta."
"To me and Marta. I'll drink to that." The boss watched him leave. He called Joey, his strong-arm bodyguard to his side.

"Follow him. He's up to something."

"Yes, boss," the bodyguard answered obediently.

Ricardo wrote to Glenda and asked her to please send more money. He told her that they are going to shut down my project! Glenda called Vladimir to tell him she got a text.

Vladimir advised, "Tell him you will have a courier bring it to him. If he doesn't accept, tell him no deal!"

Glenda contacted William by email and told him a courier would bring him the money. William said he would never get it. Glenda said to trust her. He reluctantly agreed. Vladimir prepared for his meeting with Ricardo. This time he would not escape. Glenda felt bad to know that she had to fool her internet love. However, she needed closure.

Marta went to work and worked on her marketing reports. She had accomplished a lot in one day. She had a presentation on Tuesday that had to be perfect. It was for the new company they were merging with. She worked on her charts and graphs. She worked on her marketing strategies. *I wish that relationships were as easy as this is. I can get my brain to work on charts and figures. I can't get my heart to make sense.*

She presented her presentation at the board meeting and got a bravo from the chairman. "I am glad we are coming on board with you, Marta. We will work together well."

"I believe so," Marta replied. She thanked the staff for coming. She gathered up her things and went back to her desk.

"We are having a cookout at our house, Marta. It is a meeting for only the select. Your boss, a few board members, and I are going to be there. We need to talk about the future of the company."

Glancing at her calendar, Marta asked, "Ok, when?" "We can meet next Saturday at 3:00 p.m. at my house."
"Give me directions, and I'll be there." She shook his hand. She had forgotten that Ricardo was going to take her on a trip. She belatedly remembered when she got home. She called Ricardo to tell him.

Ricardo had other pressing matters. He knew his time was running out just like what had happened to Lola. He did not want to continue to run. He wanted to be in Marta's arms once again. He remembered the sweet kisses they shared and her warm embraces.

He wanted to tell her everything about himself. He had not planned to fall in love. He had not planned that she would be such a part of his mornings. He knew that he could not live without her. However, he had to carry this internet dating through.

He planned on getting the money from the courier and heading back. He planned on buying Marta something beautiful. However, he got a call as he was heading towards the place where the courier was going to meet him. It was from Marcus. Marcus was in a panic. "They found us! I tried to get Lola out but it was too late. She's shot! You have got to come back!"

Ricardo headed towards Marcus's place and hid his car in the bushes. He watched as the boss's men were all around the property. Ricardo tried to think of what to do. The boss could not know he was in on it. He snuck around the back of the property and found some firecrackers. He lit them and threw them up in the sky.

They fell into the field near the property. The men ran over to see what the commotion was. That gave Ricardo time to get into the cabin. He heard Lola groaning, and he saw blood in the hallway. Marcus was tied up. He had been knocked out and tied up to a chair. Lola was frightened.

She was bleeding profusely from her leg. Lola pleaded, "Don't let me die like this. Not like this. I have children at home. Please help me."

"Quiet, Lola. I'll think of something." He untied Marcus. "Marcus, did you tell them anything?"
"I didn't tell them about you. Lola wouldn't give me a chance. She thought of a story of how she snuck in and hid out here."

"Then why did they tie you up?" Ricardo asked. "I don't know. Maybe they didn't like my face."

Ricardo laughed and replied, "Well I understand that!" "You're really funny, Ricardo. Hey, keep your day job!"

Ricardo was not sure what to do. The men would be coming back in and would know something was wrong. Ricardo thought of a plan. He got out his gun and shouted to the men. "Hey, I saw you caught her! I thought that was my job! What are you doing here? I was supposed to catch her!"

"Who are you?"

"I'm Ricardo! Who do you think I am? I'll take it from here." "Who sent you?" demanded the boss's men.
"Who do you think?" Ricardo answered menacingly. He sneered at them and stepped towards them with his Magnum 44 and rifle in hand.

"Don't mess with me. I can shoot both of these at the same time, and you don't want to test me in this. I've had a lot of practice!" Rattled, the men backed off.

"We'll see about this!" warned the boss's men. "Yeah, you will!" answered Ricardo. The men started coming towards Ricardo. Ricardo reacted, and they were both dead. "I told you not to test me."

Ricardo and Marcus got Lola in the car and took her to a friend who was an undercover doctor. Marcus looked at Ricardo. "Weren't you afraid?"

"No," answered Ricardo.

"You have to not care whether you live or die. When you get past that point, you're not afraid of anything. But, is there anyone whom you are afraid to see die?" Ricardo thought for a minute.

"Yes, but I won't tell you." He was thinking of Marta.

Lola began, "Ricardo, you saved me again. I can't believe you saved me." "I never intended to make a habit of it. You just keep getting into trouble. How did they find you?"

Lola answered, "I think they tapped my phone. They were able to get the signal where I was."

Ricardo thought for a minute. What if they were tracing his calls? He had to find a way to excuse where he was and what he was doing.

Vladimir was waiting at the checkpoint, and Ricardo did not show up. He called Glenda. "It was a false alarm, Glenda. He didn't show up. We have to try something else."

Glenda emailed Ricardo. "I am so sad. You didn't show up. I had all this money to give you for your project."

Ricardo answered, "I am sorry, my love. It means so much to me that you wanted to help. I will make this up to you. We can plan for another meeting. When I finish my project, I will come home to you."

"Will you really, William? Will you make it up to me?" Glenda asked hopefully.

"Yes, you know I love you, Glenda, with all my heart." Glenda read that and became angry.

She yelled at the computer. "How dare you deceive me! How dare you make me believe you loved me! You are a liar!"

But she wrote, "That's ok, dear. We will find another time so you can get the money." Ricardo was pleased she still believed him. Glenda wanted revenge and hoped she would get a chance to get retribution on him. He emailed how she would be a June bride and how he would take her away from all this.

He told her to be patient. He would be there as soon as he could. Glenda shook her head. "I can't believe I fell for his lines."

Glenda told Ricardo that she was concerned that someone had gotten into her bank account and that she was not sure if she could send more money. She said that this would be the last money she could give him. Ricardo was very concerned.

Glenda's and the other women's money helped support him. He had begun to depend on it for survival. He agreed to meet with the courier at the park at 11:00 p.m. Carry the cash in a briefcase. Glenda texted Vladimir, and he agreed. The date and the time were set. Now all Ricardo had to do was to show up, or so he thought.

Chapter 13

Katie decided she needed to do something to get away from Edward. She waited until he went to see his mother, and then she went online and found a spiritualist who could help her and give her answers.

She called and was told to come to Shady Woods Marsh in the town Mellowbrook Creek. That was an hour away. She knew that Leonardo, his son, would be out of town. He could not spy on her and get word to Edward. She got gasoline and headed down the road.

The spiritualist, whose name was Lela, met Katie at the door. She offered her some tea.

"I have news for you, Katie Valashi. Your days are numbered. You have a man that will try to end your life. You need to get your things together. I foresee that he will take you by the hair, pull you down, and put his hands around your throat. This will not be the only time. There will come a time where he will threaten to kill you or have someone else do it. You need to decide what your means of escape will be. This is in your near future. How you survive this is in your hands!"

"What will I do?" Katie wept uncontrollably.

Putting an arm around Katie, the spiritualist declared, "You need to stay strong. Make a plan of escape. When he comes back, you are in danger. Every minute you are near him could be your death!"

Pitifully, Katie cried, "But, I love him! How can I leave?"

With an understanding smile, Lela solemnly predicted, "Then you will remain with him until death parts you. The choice is yours. Do not go back."

Shaking her head, Katie declared, "I have to! He will surely find me!"

"As you wish. That will be $50.00, Katie." Katie handed her the money and walked away. What if she was right? She knew that Edward was still with his mother. Katie was still recovering from the bruises he had given her.

She stopped by to see her pastor and told him what had been happening and that she got some advice from a spiritualist that Edward was going to kill her.

I am so frightened! I don't know what to do. Edward spent all my inheritance!

Pastor Mark prayed and said, Katie, I am glad that you came by to see me. I have been concerned about your safety. God has a better plan for your life. Pastor Mark talked about Jesus and about His plan and purpose that can be rediscovered by restoring fellowship with Him, through faith in Jesus Christ.

Katie prayed and cried with her pastor and rededicated her life to Christ. Pastor Mark warned Katie that she needed to go to the police.

Pastor Mark gave Katie a bible and walked her to her car. Pastor Mark said, "This will help you as you face your fears."

"Thank you," said Katie. He recommended Katie go to the police station. They will know where the closest women's shelter is. Katie got into her car and felt God's angels surrounding her. She felt stronger than she had in years.

She had to get home before Edward's son Leonardo found out where she was. She stopped by the police station and asked for help. Morris, a middle-aged policeman, listened to her story and took pictures of her bruises. He took notes and said that he would bring Edward into custody.

He escorted her to a place of safety. He told her not to go home. Katie had never been in a shelter before. She did not know what to expect. The door opened, and she walked in.

Glenda waited by her phone to get the text of where Vladimir was going to meet William Monroe. William responded back to Vladimir on his phone by texting.

He said to meet him in the city square. He said he only needed $2,000.00 to finish the project.

Then he would come home to her. Ricardo had promised himself this was the last time he would ask Glenda for money. Glenda called Vladimir regarding how much money he had to bring.

Vladimir had a suitcase full of money for the bait. Ricardo arrived at 11 p.m., but after waiting 15 minutes, there was no sign of the courier. He was about to leave when a man showed up with a black coat and hat.

His face was covered, so he was not recognizable. "Are you the courier?" "Yes, I am. Are you William Monroe?"

"Yes! Where's the cash?" Vladimir handed the suitcase over to him. William opened it up. It had $2,000.00 in unmarked bills.

Ricardo started walking away with the suitcase. Vladimir called after him. "Not so fast. Anything you want to tell Glenda?"

Ricardo thought for a moment and then answered, "Tell her I was not the one for her. Better luck next time."

Immediately, Vladimir answered, "That's what I thought you would say, Ricardo!"

"What! How did you know who I was?" Vladimir took off his mask and revealed his true identity.

"I told you I would get my revenge, Ricardo. Karma is a bitch, isn't it?" Ricardo tried to run, but Vladimir had backups that handcuffed him.

Ricardo said, "You can't do that! You have to read me my Miranda rights."

Vladimir answered, "We're not cops, Ricardo. We are your worst nightmare. I am FBI. You are going to have to answer for all your crimes."

He showed Ricardo his badge. "What crimes?" Ricardo inquired.

"Let's try wrongful impersonation, fraud, extortion, and murder." Struggling to extricate himself from the handcuffs,

Ricardo declared, "You can't prove this!" yelled Ricardo. "Yes, I can," said Vladimir. "You can tell it to your attorney! Put him in the car!"

Glenda waited by her phone to hear from Vladimir. She wanted to believe that William Monroe was still a good person and that he had loved her. She lay on her bed and watched the fan spin. She wondered how she had ever become so vulnerable and lonely. By now she should be married with four kids. Instead, she went to work, hoping for some excitement in her life. Well, she got some excitement. Just not the kind she expected.

She started writing a song. She finished writing and sat down at her piano and played. Her fingers bounced off the keys to the sad melody. She wondered where she would go from here. He had taken everything and left nothing of her behind.

She sang, "I pray for peace. I pray for love. I pray for hope and guidance Ricardo realized he had been playing all the time. Marta shook her head.
"All the time you were chasing me, you never guessed who I was. You didn't even realize that it wasn't really my aunt who talked to you. She was another agent. You are not as smart as you thought you were. Tell us who your boss is. We will change your identity. They will never be able to find you." Ricardo looked out the window and saw that some of his boss's men were looking for him.

"Right," Ricardo smirked. "They will never find me."

Just then, gunshots hit the window. Marta was a marksman shooter. She pointed her rifle at one of the boss's men and gave a warning shot that parted one of the men's hair.

"Next time you won't be so lucky!" said Marta. "Remind me to never piss you off!" said Ricardo.

"Ok, this is your last warning, Ricardo! Get away from the window!" Marta got Ricardo out of sight.

Vladimir called for backup. Other agents were called in to surround the building and catch the men who were after Ricardo. Vladimir caught one of them, but the other escaped. He brought him in for questioning. "Ricardo, you're a dead man! What did you tell them?"

"Nothing. I don't know anything." "Good. Keep it that way!" Thinking quickly, Ricardo asked, "Marta, what do I need to do?"

"You work with us. You can get your name cleared and your identity changed. You will be like the man without a face. You will be a shadow. It's your choice. Or, we can throw you back on the streets."

"No, I'll work with you. Either way, I'm dead." Ricardo told what he knew. He had been doing this job for 20 years. The rules from the boss were getting tougher. He didn't know whom to trust. He knew this boss from a gang he was with as a teenager. His boss defended him from the other guys.

He told them that the boss was his hero and that he had taught him how to fight and shoot a gun. He was like the father he never had. He then told them how his boss had changed the last few years and had forced him to kill people that the boss didn't like or couldn't trust.

Ricardo ended by saying, "Now they're hunting me." "You are under witness protection now."

Marta replied reassuringly. "Plus, I know a surgeon who can change your looks so they cannot recognize you."

Meanwhile, one of the men got back to the boss and told him that Joey and Ricardo were caught. The boss told his man to watch headquarters to see if they would be taken to a safe place.

The boss declared, "I don't care what it takes. He is not going to destroy what I built up here! Whatever it takes!"

The boss left the room and slammed the door. Vladimir came back to headquarters and sought out Ricardo. "I found a place where they cannot find you. You can go where you will be safe."

Anxiously, Ricardo answered, "No place is safe now. Where are you taking me?" "You'll see soon enough," Vladimir replied.
"It will be a place they would never expect and you won't recognize." Vladimir gave Ricardo a drink to calm his nerves. Everything got dark and fuzzy. Ricardo dropped to the floor.

When Ricardo woke up, he was lying in a hospital bed with an IV in his arm. Everything looked fuzzy. He looked around. He was in a private room. He blinked and tried to focus. Marta walked into the room.

"Oh, you're up! How did you sleep?"

"Where am I? How did I get here?" asked Ricardo.

"You are asking too many questions. You need to get some rest." "I don't want to rest! Where am I?"
"You will know soon enough," Marta replied.

"Don't worry. I will be back. I will get you some lunch."

Ricardo was panicking and trying to calm himself down. "I have to get out of here."

He pulled the IV out of his arm and tried to get up. He had trouble moving. He held onto the bed and tried to walk towards the mirror. Something did not seem right. His face felt itchy like there was something on it. He was afraid to look.

He scooted one foot at a time towards the mirror. He held onto the sink and slowly looked up. He looked at his face and screamed in horror. His face was bandaged up. He was unrecognizable. He was afraid to remove the bandages and to see what was done to him. He held onto a stand and scooted towards the bed. He fell down on the bed. He wondered what to do.

Vladimir came into the room. "Ricardo, we need to have a talk. You will never look the same. This is for your protection. You are going to have a different name and face. From now on, you will start a new life. You will work for me. You know a lot about the inside of crime. We will stop the syndicates in their tracks! You will be like a shadow. They will not know when you are there or when you go."

"Don't I have a say?" Ricardo asked.

"Yes, you do. You can leave and be a free man with no identity or money. Or, you can get paid and work for me."

Ricardo could feel the anesthetic wearing off and started to feel intense pain. "It's going to take some time for you to recover. Lay down before you fall down," Vladimir encouraged. Ricardo tried to lie down. The nurse came in and put the IV back in his arm.

He started to fall asleep again. "Get your rest now, Ricardo. Working for me, you're going to need it."

Chapter 14

Katie checked in at the shelter. All she had was her purse, her sweater, and a water bottle. She checked in and was assigned her room. She looked around. The woman at the shelter said, "Are you Katie? The officer told us you were coming."

"Yes, I am Katie."

The woman at the shelter advised of the support groups and help groups available. Katie no longer felt alone. She did not know what her next steps would be. She was assigned a room. She walked into the room and lay down. She finally went to sleep. She attended a support group the next day and met another woman who had been abused.

When it was her turn to speak, she said, "We sit near the TV, watching a show. We sit in the same room, and yet, we're apart. We do not talk. We savor the silence. No words can end the sadness I feel. So we go through a routine, and we do what's expected. I feel so alone. I want to yell out for us to stop the madness!' I need you! I need to love you. I don't want to be without you! Instead, I sit in silence and wait for him to make the next move. We watch TV, but my heart is dying. I wonder sometimes, can he hear me? Can he feel me shaking inside? I need to feel that I matter to him. What does he feel? When we are close, I feel so strong. When we are mad at each other, I feel so weak and empty. I want to ask him to please love me again. I want him to hold me like he has never held me. I need to feel loved and safe."

One of the women asked, "What has he done to you? I can see you still love him."

Katie started crying. Between sobs, she continued, "He beats and abuses me where no one can see. I am afraid of him. I am afraid of what he will do to me. He does not care if he kills or hurts someone like me. He is cruel, hurtful, and will not show love or be kind. God only knows if he is having sex with someone else. Yet he accuses me of being with someone else. He never thinks of me. He thinks of himself. He never cares or knows how mean he really is.

I am so afraid of him."

She started crying uncontrollably. The other ladies listened and told their stories. Katie started to realize that she was not alone. She started feeling safe for the first time.

Chapter 15

The boss checked to see where they had taken Ricardo. No one was able to determine his whereabouts. The boss warned, "If he squeals, he's dead. I should have never trusted that kid. Call whoever you can to trace where they took Ricardo."

"Who do we call?"

"That's not my problem. That's yours! Just find him."

The boss started thinking. What would it take to get Ricardo to not tell anything about his involvement? He would try to get Marta!

The boss asked, "Where is she playing next?"

His men replied, "She will be playing at the amphitheater in Mariner Hill. We'll be waiting!"

Marta practiced for her set. She drove to the amphitheater and played. She sang the song she had written for Ricardo. She even sang "The final goodbye."

She got a little teary eyed remembering how he had sung it to her. She got a standing ovation from the crowd and was asked to come back and sing. After her set, she started walking towards her car with her guitar in hand. There was a thug in her car who grabbed her from behind.

She dropped her guitar and practiced some of her black belt techniques she learned in the FBI. She knocked him out. There were others that were trying to get her. She put her key in the ignition, threw her guitar in, and noticed the ignition started making a grinding sound.

Come on, come on! Finally, it started up just as other men were trying to break into the car. She turned the car around, and they fell to the ground. She raced out, and her heart was beating fast. They are on to me. I've got to get out of here! She drove as fast as she could and was able to get off on a side road. The boss's men went straight.

She called Vladimir and told him what had happened.

"Are you all right?" he asked anxiously.

"Yes, but they're on to me. I have to watch being out in public," Marta replied. "You're right," Vladimir agreed. "But how did you do?"
Patting her guitar, Marta surmised, "I did well. I got a standing ovation." "I'm not surprised," answered Vladimir. "You are good at what you do."
Marta smiled but then replied, "I am just hoping I didn't hurt my guitar. It is my most cherished possession."

"Don't worry," answered Vladimir. "If it's broken, I'll get you another."

Marta shook her head. "You don't understand. You can't replace what someone has given you."

Marta thought about how her dad had taught her the guitar. He was a classical guitar player. He taught her how to play like a performer, not just an amateur. He taught her how to be confident in the face of criticism and sarcasm. He taught her how to be proud of herself and who she was.

Most of all, he taught her how to have a love of music. He held the guitar like it was a precious gift. He took care of the body, the neck, and the strings. He played it like it was the only musical instrument on the planet. How she loved to hear him play. Before he died, he called her to him and urged her to take care of the guitar. Treat it gently.

If you do, you will get many years of joy. You will bring joy to many people. If Dad had known I had to throw the guitar case down to fight off attackers, I wonder what he would have thought. Somehow, I think he would have understood. She checked the guitar. It was still in perfect condition. God bless a good guitar case!

She went to the hospital room to check on Ricardo. He was awake. She sat on the bed beside him.

"I am sorry this had to happen to you, Ricardo. You don't know what we went through to get you here. You were like dead weight in the back of the car. We had to keep you down so no one could see you leave. Finally we ditched them and brought you here."

The doctor came in. "Ricardo, you can now remove your bandages." Ricardo ruefully replied, "I am not sure if I want to." In a reassuring voice, the doctor replied, "I think you will like what you see."

He removed the bandages, and he looked permanently like the movie star from the 40's he had chosen to imitate. He gasped.

"Now, Ricardo, you will have the perfect face. You need the perfect name. Shall we call you William?"

"That's very funny."

"Then how about we call you Bill?"

"Bill is ok. Bill would grow on me. Bill Monroe it is." The matter was decided.
Marta held Ricardo close to her side. "Don't worry. You will always be my Ricardo. You are just Bill Monroe to everyone else. You know, they will recognize you. You needed to change your appearance."

"I can do that. I will miss performing with you, Marta, but I can do that as long as I am in this town. What should we do now, Marta?"

"Well, we have to think about what we are going to do. We can't stay here."

"I know. But where should we go? The boss has connections everywhere! It's only a matter of time before they catch up with us."

Marta replied, "We are flying to California. I have some friends who will take us in."

Ricardo remarked, "I've always wanted to go to California."

"Well, then, you will get your wish. It is the last place they will think of looking for us."

"You don't know how powerful he is, Marta. I know you and I are an irresistible force. We are a force to be reckoned with!"

She gave him a gentle kiss. "As long as we're together, I know everything is going to be alright."

Smiling serenely, Marta replied, "I believe that too, Ricardo." She lay beside him on the hospital bed. He wrapped his arms around her and went to sleep. When they woke up, the doctor said that Ricardo had a clean bill of health and that he could go.

Vladimir took them to the airport. "Are you sure about this, Marta? I could make a good life for you here."

"I have made my choice, Vladimir. He's the one."

Vladimir gave her a kiss goodbye and helped her board the plane. "You better be good to her, Ricardo. I will be watching."

Ricardo replied, "I will take care of her. Don't worry." "I'm worrying already!" sighed Vladimir.
They got on the flight, and Vladimir waved goodbye. He was misty-eyed thinking about Marta. He wished she had made a different choice. Why would she choose Ricardo?

The flight was divided into 2 sections. One was a small plane with hardly enough room to move around. They had a two-hour layover. They stopped and had a snack at the airport deli. People stared at him.

"Ricardo," she whispered, "you do look like a movie star! Even so, they keep staring!"

Laughing, Ricardo inquired, "Do I start signing autographs?"

Marta answered, "No, just look natural." He smiled and winked his eyes at the ladies. They swooned as he walked by. He jokingly observed, "You know, I might start to like this!"

"Remember you're with me now. I know who you really are!"

"Yes, dear, I will do whatever you say," Ricardo obediently answered. They checked in for their second flight to California. Their flight landed in San Francisco.

Her friends greeted her with open arms. "It is so good to see you! Let me get your bags."

"That's ok. It's so good to see you."

"Are any shows performing?" Marta excitedly asked.

"Not yet. But you can be my headliner!" Marta was excited. She had waited her whole life to perform in San Francisco.

"Are you William?" her friends inquired. "Yes, but you can call me Bill."
"Hi, Bill. I bet you got some jet lag being on the plane for so long. BTW, do you play any golf?"

Ricardo replied, "I haven't for a while. But I have watched Caddyshack. Does that count?"

"Not hardly, but I will help you brush up on your strokes."

They went into downtown San Francisco and got on a cable car to Fisherman's Wharf. They ate fresh fish, sourdough bread, and baked potatoes. Marta caught them up on all the news.

She talked about the high-speed chase with the car and how Ricardo had changed his identity. She then talked about how she broke up with Vladimir and how jealous he had become. Most of all, she talked about how glad she was to be home.

"How long are you staying?" Marta's friends asked.

"We're not sure yet. We'll stay 'till the smoke clears and they forget about us."

Ricardo interjected, "How can they forget about you, Marta? Unforgettable is what you are…"

Laughing, Marta replied, "Watch out, family and friends, he's breaking into a song again…"

They got back on the cable car and got in the car towards her friends' home. "You're going to love San Francisco. You're never going to want to leave."

Ricardo observed, "I want to have a normal life eventually."

Marta's friends answered, "That's going to take some time. You have had to make some big adjustments. If anybody can help you, it's Marta!"

Marta gave him a hug. "Don't worry. You are safe. This is a different town than you have known. We protect each other on the streets. We have our own connections."

Sleepily, Ricardo replied, "I would love to hear about it. However, right now, I am ready to fall asleep."

Her friends showed Marta and William their room. They snuggled close and fell asleep.

Marta woke up to the smell of coffee brewing. Ricardo was still asleep. She put her robe on and went into the kitchen.

"How did you sleep?" her friend Nadine asked. "Hmm, I slept like a baby," answered Marta. "Want some coffee?" asked Nadine. "Love some. I am letting him sleep."

"Just as well," Nadine observed. "It gives us time to talk. Marta, are you sure this is what you want? You don't really know him. He is a dangerous man. He has people after him. You could have anyone you want."

Firmly, Marta answered, "I want him. He is the one I have been looking for all my life."

"Marta, think of the decision you are making. You are still young.

Please give this some thought. He could take you down with him!"

Seeking to reassure her friend, Marta replied, "I know it doesn't make sense. My mind tells me that he is not good for me. Yet, my heart tells me he is the one."

Shaking her head, Nadine chided, "Marta, you are not thinking straight. Here, have some more coffee." She sat at the table and enjoyed the aroma of fresh-ground coffee beans in a cup. She added Kona to her coffee. It had Columbian coffee beans that her friend had ground for her. All in all, it was a great cup of coffee. William came into the kitchen and politely asked, "May I have some coffee?"

Nadine offered, "Here, pour you a cup."

"Thanks," said William. "Marta and I were just talking about her future. What do you see happening, William?"

"I see myself marrying Marta and us having a happy life."

Marta looked at William. Nadine rolled her eyes. "I'm sorry I asked. This is getting too deep for me here." Nadine went into the living room. William and Marta looked at each other and held hands.

"Is that really what you want, Ricardo?" "Yes, more than anything." Marta didn't know what to say...

The boss had heard that Ricardo had left town. He checked with the airports on boarding flights where Ricardo would have flown anywhere. There was no Ricardo on any of the flights in the last two months. Then he must have changed his name. Wherever Marta is, he will not be far behind.

They checked the airlines. There was a Marta who flew out of town a month before, according to the boss's sources. They were not able to get information on where because of federal regulations. We will find him. We will find both of them!

Vladimir had his people looking out for Marta. He called her. He told her that there were people looking for her.

"Be careful!" Vladimir urged. "How long are you going to be there?" Marta answered, "We are planning to come back in a couple of days." "Just to let you know," said Vladimir, "your home was ransacked. I am taking care of Biscuit till you come back. You need to get her so she doesn't keep peeing on the floor."

"Poor Biscuit! She's scared!" cried Marta. "She doesn't know where I am, and she misses her momma!"

"Poor Biscuit? Poor me!" answered Vladimir. "Ricardo, or shall I say William, ends up with the beauty, and I end up with the dog. Something's wrong here!"

"Ha! Ha! Vladimir," answered Marta. Vladimir smirked, "That's not funny. That's my life!"

"I still love you too, Vladimir. I just love him more."

"I don't get it," reasoned Vladimir. "I can provide a better life for you. I can take care of you. What does he have to offer? He only has love."

"That's all I need," sighed Marta. "I don't understand women. You could have it all, and you settle for less," complained Vladimir.

"Give Biscuit my love," asked Marta. Vladimir hung up the phone. He petted Biscuit on the head. Biscuit licked his face and relieved herself on the floor.

"Not a good trade-off, Biscuit. One of us needs to go." Biscuit looked at him with her sweet brown puppy eyes. "Well, I guess we both stay. Biscuit, what do you want to watch on TV?"

Biscuit snuggled next to Vladimir. "Let's watch an action adventure!" Biscuit was happy with that decision. She barked in approval.

William looked in Marta's eyes and saw sadness but yet sincerity. "I have never met anyone like you. I need to confess something. I have a mission I need to finish. It might take time. But you will be in my heart every step of the way."

"But you just met me," she replied.

"No, I feel I have known you all my life. You are the woman I have been destined to meet."

Marta could hear in the back of her mind a sarcastic phrase to his comment. Marta still didn't trust Ricardo.

However, she enjoyed being with him. She was living in the moment. They talked till 2:00 p.m. She told him that it was getting late. He held her close and gently urged, "Stay with me. Be my bride. I will take care of you, and all your bills will be paid."

All she could think of was "Who would keep my dog?"

He laughed. "I will treat your dog like my own," he promised. They listened to a song and danced. He held her close. He kissed her. She had to ask. "Why are you pursuing me?"

Ricardo replied, "Because I am your Bruce Wayne, and you are my Cat woman. We are the other parts of each other, destined to meet." Even if it were just in make believe, she was happy to just hold him close.

Glenda called Vladimir. The phone rang twice, and Vladimir picked up. "Hello?"

"Hello, Vladimir. This is Glenda. I don't know what to do. William Monroe really messed up my banking accounts. I can't pay my bills. If I don't do something soon, I will have to declare bankruptcy."

Vladimir replied, "I'm sorry, Glenda. But you trusted him. We can't recover the money you sent. It will be on you."

"But you know it was William Monroe that did this," Glenda insisted. "He gave the information to his boss, and he set up these accounts..."

Vladimir replied, "You chose to give your banking information to him. Unfortunately, this happens too often. These people come across as saving the world but they are out for their own profit. You will be responsible for the funds lost or over drafted from your account."

"Are you sure there is nothing you can do?" cried Glenda. "I'm sorry," Vladimir consoled.
"There is nothing. You are out of luck." Glenda started crying.

"Then I will file bankruptcy. Whatever happened to helping the victim?" Glenda hung up. She lay on her bed and stared at the fan.

"My life's over. I don't know what to do now." She called a bankruptcy attorney and made an appointment.

Vladimir said to himself, "If I only knew who the boss was, we could recover those funds. Ricardo won't tell us. Why can't Marta get him to tell us?"

Chapter 16

In the meantime, Marta was having problems of her own. Ricardo was not happy living in San Francisco. They were starting to argue. Money was running low.
She was having problems paying the bills.

She called Vladimir. "I need to come back and start working again. I have no other choice. Ricardo, or Bill Monroe, as he now calls himself, doesn't want to do anything but lie on the couch. He is depressed. I am frustrated! He has become more of a problem than a help. It's time to come back."

Vladimir was happy to hear that. He had been waiting for her to listen to reason. She booked tickets for Toxic Love her and Ricardo (Bill) back home.

Vladimir promised that he would pick them up at the airport. "Marta, we have to get a resolution to this case. Glenda called and said she would have to file bankruptcy because of William Monroe. I told her I could not help her. Marta, you can help her by finding out who the boss is. Then we can recover the funds."

Marta replied, "We aren't really talking. Maybe you can get it out of him. Whatever it takes, Vladimir, do it. You were right all the time."

Vladimir answered, "I didn't want to say I told you so, but I did tell you…"

"I know, I know. You were right. Our flight is on American Airlines flight 6073 coming in at 9:00 a.m. tomorrow."

"I will be there. Do you think you can part with Ricardo for a while?"
"I would be glad to! He's yours after this!"

"Does he know you feel this way?" "Not yet, but he will! "Good, the less he knows the better. I'll see you at 9:00 a.m."

"I will see you later!" Marta hung up. Ricardo came in. "Who were you talking to?"

"Vladimir. I need to get back. My vacation is over, and I need to go back to work. We have tickets for an early flight tomorrow. We will get in at 9:00 a.m."

"Good! Life will go back to normal!" replied Ricardo. "You've got that right!" said Marta.

From her grandfather, who had given the boat to her? She secured the boat and trailer to the car and then drove to the dock. The traffic wasn't bad for a Saturday. Ricardo helped her back up the truck onto the dock, and Marta got the boat into the water and tied the boat to the deck. Ricardo parked the truck.

Marta got into the boat. She untied the rope to the boat and pulled up the anchor. They set sail. She and Ricardo put on their life vests. It was a beautiful day with a deep blue sky. There were other people jet skiing. Ricardo jumped in the water.

The water was cold, almost icy. He shivered and came up for air. He put on his water skis. He held on tight to the rope. He put on the water skis and tied them. He nodded to Marta that he was ready to ski.

Marta nodded her head and went full power. He was up on top of the water. He laughed. This was fun! He held onto the rope, and Marta started going faster.
Ricardo was enjoying watching the waves of the water and feeling the summer sun on his face. She did donuts in the water, seeing if he could keep up. He met the challenge.

Marta saw a boat in the distance. Some of the people looked familiar from profiles at headquarters. Marta was right. The boss had sent their lookouts to follow Marta. They got out their binoculars and looked at the boats in the harbor. They had already scoped out Marta's boat and seen a man skiing.

They took pictures on their phones and sent them to the boss. The boss replied, "Well, he is pretending to be William Monroe. No wonder we could not find him. Thanks, Marta. You made this too easy for me."

He called Gilbert, one of his men, to rent a Jet Ski. Gilbert found a place where he could rent a Jet Ski by the hour and then untied the ski from the dock. He grabbed the keys from the dashboard. Then he started the motor. He had the Jet Ski tied up to the dock; he shifted it from neutral to forward. Before he knew it, he was catching up to the boat. He took more pictures with his camera and asked the boss what was the next step.

The boss said, "Follow the boat and see where it goes. Don't look too obvious. Play it cool." Marta got a bad feeling about the men on the other boat. She told Ricardo to get in the boat. He was not listening.

She yelled, "Get in the boat! You need to get in the boat!" This time he heard her. "What's wrong, Marta?"

"I recognize the people in that boat. I think they might be some of the people who are looking for you." Ricardo looked towards the left and saw some familiar faces. He motioned for Marta to go faster.

Marta tried to go faster and noticed one of the boss's men started to follow them on a Jet Ski. He started shooting towards Ricardo. Ricardo tried to decide what to do. Then he realized how many tough situations he had gotten himself out of. He realized what he was capable of at the right moment. He jumped a wave in a low position on the skis.

He quickly pushed the skis off his feet. After he fell, he realized that the boat was going to turn around to get him. Gilbert, who was racing along on his Jet Ski, was turning around to where he fell. Ricardo wrestled to get the skis off his feet. He got a big gulp of air and swam underwater to a nearby pier.

Ricardo knew Gilbert could not see him. He was swimming fast underwater. He started swimming towards a pier. He let go of the rope and dived into the water. The man on the Jet Ski turned his ski around and started looking for Ricardo near the pier. Ricardo had dived far enough down where the man could not see him.

When Ricardo saw that Gilbert was looking for him, he held onto the pier. He tried to hide under the pier where no one could see him. Gilbert rode the Jet Ski close to the pier but did not see or find

Ricardo. He tied up the Jet Ski to the pier and continued his search.

Gilbert looked around the dock where he had seen Ricardo. Ricardo held his breath and tried to hide from view. Marta cried out for Ricardo. She saw Ricardo and exclaimed, "Ricardo, you're safe!"

Gilbert saw Ricardo holding onto the pier. He knocked him back into the water. Gilbert hit Ricardo, but Ricardo hit back. Gilbert was holding him down so he couldn't come up for air and eventually knocked him out.

He called the other men on the boat to get Ricardo. Gilbert said, "The boss wants to see you personally. He said he wants you alive."

Ricardo knew that his days were numbered. The boss had said what would happen if he was ever crossed.

Ricardo to lead them off your trail. "However, there is nothing I can do until I get there. I will call the border patrol and see if they can catch the boss' men. Marta, I thought you were more careful than this."

"Vladimir, I feel bad enough. That's enough!" cried Marta.

Vladimir asked Marta to give any details about the men and the boat they were on. She told them it was a tourist-looking boat with men with machine guns.

Vladimir called the border patrol.

They said they would be looking for the boat. Vladimir assured Marta that he would catch a flight to San Francisco and would do what he could to help resolve this case. The boat was already out of sight by the time the border patrol came.
There was no sign of Ricardo anywhere.

Chapter 17

Ricardo woke up in a bed in a cheap hotel. The boss's men stood around him with guns. The boss was standing over him.

"Well, Ricardo? We will meet again." "Yes," said Ricardo.
"It seems like I wake up in the darndest places. I am afraid to sleep anymore." "So, Ricky, you have a lot of explaining to do."

"That's very funny, boss." Ricardo told the boss how he was kidnapped, drugged, and how they changed his face. He told them how they did not know who the boss was. He made sure. He told them how the FBI was trying to force him to give information and how he had lied about everything.

"Ricardo, I know you. You have been like a son to me. I want to know why you protected Lola. You know she betrayed me. Then you saved her life. Lucky for you, that last gunshot killed her. Your friend is not in good shape either. He didn't know who you were. He was just being a Good Samaritan because she was a woman who needed help."

"I'm sorry, boss. She was like an aunt to me. That's why I protected her."

"Where is your loyalty? Where do you think Marta's loyalty is? Do you think she loves you more than her commitment to her job? Even now she is betraying you. Did you know what has been going on with her and Vladimir? And you still believed her?"

"Yes, I did. But I would rather work for you again, boss. At least I know what to expect. She is hot and cold at the same time. I can't figure her out."

The boss laughed. "Did you ever expect to? Ricardo, are you sure you want to keep that false face?"

Ricardo replied, "Your original plan was to temporarily change my face. You were more of a friend than she was."

The boss laughed. "You are right as always. At least when I had my face changed, it was not permanent."

I will have our plastic surgeon to turn you back into Ricardo. You need to get back to Glenda and the other ladies. They are waiting to give you money."

Ricardo replied, "Oh yeah! That's right!"

The boss continued, "While you have this face, talk to them again. Call them and tell them how you miss them. By all means, tell them if they send money you will meet them in the summer."

"Ok, boss. I will."

"Good boy. You are finally learning who is on your side and who isn't."

Ricardo texted Glenda and asked her forgiveness for not contacting her. He told her that he had been busy working on the project. He would make it up to her. He begged her to send money.

He told her that he didn't appreciate her having a fake courier and that he wouldn't love her if she did that again. He told her that he loved her. He realized that he couldn't live without her.

Glenda wanted to believe him. She contacted the other ladies and told them the same thing. He emailed Katherine, another person he met on the internet. He asked her to set up a bank account.

Then he said that he would need the bank account information. He said that he would also need her social security number. He advised that he needed these funds for his project. Everyone believed him but Glenda. She told him that she knew he was lying and would not send money to him.

He said that was all right as long as she loved him. She told him that you don't love unless someone gives you money or account information. He thought about that and realized part of that was true. Even Marta had a catch. Everyone had something they wanted.

He said, "Glenda, if I didn't ask you for money, can you see a life with you and me? Can you forgive me where you wouldn't look back at our past? Can you ever forgive the bad things I've done and love me again?"

Glenda thought about it and felt sad. She could forgive, but she didn't know if she could ever forget. There had been too much damage to her heart and to her faith in him.

"Glenda, you are the only one I know that doesn't want anything from me. You just want to love me. I want to love you too. When I come back to the States, I want to marry you." Glenda did not reply. Her heart still hurts from all his lies and deceit. Ricardo told her to "think it over." He replied with love and kisses at the bottom of his text.

Glenda realized he was right that everyone had a catch. She hoped that Ricardo had changed and that he realized her true value. Glenda's common sense told her that he hadn't learned a thing. She called her sister Joanie in New Jersey and told her what had happened.

Joanie couldn't believe that her sister would fall for someone like William (Ricardo). "Don't you believe you can just meet a guy on your own without the internet?" asked Joanie.

"That's easy for you to say. You have five kids and a happy marriage. I have two dogs and a parakeet."

"Well, you have to sing wherever you go." "You're funny, Joanie. Don't forget to keep your day job."

"Don't worry; I will. By the way, Donald says hi!"

"Yeah, tell your husband I said hello. He is a lucky guy." "No, I'm a lucky woman, and I know it."
Glenda asked about the kids and how Little League was going. She asked about what was going on in the community. She asked about what Joanie did for fun.

Joanie said, "With five kids, a job, and taking care of the home, I have fun taking a warm bath or having a few moments to read and have a cup of tea. I am always busy with the kids' activities."

"I envy you, Joanie. You have the kind of life I always wanted to have."

"Glenda, you still can. Don't give up. Don't settle for less." Glenda said goodbye and thought about what Joanie had said.

Chapter 18

"I had a feeling that you would be coming," replied Pastor Browning. "That is why I called for backup. The police will be here any second."

Katie had not realized that the pastor had called the police while she was going outside. "You have nothing on me. That is my wife."

"I have seen the bruises and scars," replied Pastor Browning, "and oh, yes, I do." Edward started fuming and cursing. "You better come home, Katie!"
He got in his car and left. Katie was trembling. "You saved me! You really protected me!"

"No one is going to hurt you again," assured Pastor Browning.

"I am taking you to the police station, and I want you to file formal charges. Men like him need to be behind bars."

He drove her to the police station. She wrote her report. "What about my car?"

"I will have someone pick it up for you," Pastor Browning replied. "Thank you! How can I ever repay you?"

Wisely, Pastor Browning counseled, "Learn who Jesus really is. He will be the greatest friend you ever had."

He handed her a Bible and then drove her back to the shelter. "This is quite a story to tell in a group!" exclaimed Katie.

Glenda decided that she would write William Monroe one more time. She told him that if he was serious about her, he needed to meet her. She told him where, when, how, and what time. Ricardo gave it some thought and talked to the boss.

"If I meet with her, she will believe me."

"All right, Ricardo. Tell her where you will meet her. Play along."

William Monroe (Ricardo) agreed to meet Glenda and arranged a romantic rendezvous with her. He said he would take her to a villa in Italy. He told her to pack her bags. He would take her to Venice so he could serenade her with his mandolin and sing sweet love songs that made her heart dance.

Glenda told William, "If it gets any deeper, I am going to need higher boots."

William tried to reassure her by saying, "If you don't believe me, you will never know if it will happen. I will meet you at the airport at 2:00 p.m. Our plane leaves at 4:00 p.m."

Glenda's heart danced, but she still did not believe it was possible. Her heart kept telling her, "What if?"

Her mind kept telling her, "What are you doing?" She decided to give him another chance. She was at the airport at 1:45 p.m. She told herself that he probably won't show up.

At 2:00 p.m., sharp, William Monroe came into the airport. He walked up to her, smiled, and asked if she was ready for the flight. He had hers and his tickets.

She said, "Let's have a coffee and talk first."

"Glenda, there will be a long checkout line. We have to go."

Refusing to budge, Glenda replied, "Let's get coffee first. We need to talk." "Ok, we'll talk," Ricardo agreed.
"I know who you are. You are not really William Monroe. You are someone named Ricardo. That is just a face you put on for me."

William replied, "Oh, yeah? Then try to take off my mask!" She touched his skin and realized him. He needed someone he could count on. That would be Glenda.

They stopped at the Heathrow Airport in London to change flights. Then they had a two-hour layover in London. He took her to a nearby pub. She walked hand and hand with William. She got a chance to see a few of the nearby sights. Then it was time to go. They flew to Venice. The plane stopped, and they got their bags.

William had reserved a hotel in a nice area in Venice. They stopped for a cappuccino. It started raining. Glenda did not mind. She had William by her side.

"Glenda, since we are alone, there is something I must tell you. I am Ricardo. I have realized that I love you far beyond the rest. You have a gentle heart and spirit."

Gently taking her hand, he said, "This weekend you will come first. You will be the only one I see."
Glenda replied, "Are you sure? Can you give up the life you had?"
"No," Ricardo replied, "but you come with my life."
He gave her a kiss. "Glenda, I will keep you safe. No harm will come to you when I am around."

Glenda gave him a kiss. "I want so much to believe you, but I can't."
Ricardo looked at her sternly. "Then why did you come if you don't believe me?"

Ricardo found a wedding chapel. He told Glenda he had a wedding dress picked out for her made of the finest lace. She went into a side room and put on the dress and shoes. She looked like an angel. Ricardo put on a suit with a fancy tie. He looked dashing and handsome. He placed his hands in hers and asked the chaplain to say the vows.

Ricardo looked in her eyes and asked her to marry him. She said, "I do."
Ricardo said "I do" too and gave her a passionate kiss. They bowed at the altar and took their vows. He took her on a beautiful canoe ride and pretended he was the gondolier. Then he took her to a restaurant and had a romantic dinner.

They spent the night in each other's arms and fell asleep. "Glenda, I finally know what I have been looking for. I like adventure, but more than anything I want a woman with a big heart. That has always been you."

She said, "Down in my heart I always knew that." They kissed and said goodnight.

Chapter 19

The next morning, Ricardo made the coffee. He made a breakfast of eggs with hollandaise sauce. He had French toast with real butter and assorted fruit in a bowl. He poured orange juice. Glenda woke with the smell of coffee and amazing aromas from the kitchen.

"Good morning, sweetheart." He gave her a kiss and a hug.

"This is my special treat for you." He had the table set with roses in a vase. He pulled out her chair and had her sit down. He poured her coffee. Then he served her breakfast. He put a plate down for himself and sat down next to her. They started eating breakfast. Glenda replied, "Is there anything you can't do well?"

"Yes, but you will never have to find out." Glenda smiled and drank her coffee. He said, "Glenda, my job can be dangerous at times. But now that I will be coming home it was really him.

"Now do you believe me? Will you give our love one more try?" He kissed her.

"Let's go, Glenda. We need to make up for lost time. There is a beautiful wedding chapel in Venice. We can go to Rome for our honeymoon."

Glenda could not believe that he would really marry her. They went through the checkout line and checked in their bags.

Then they went through the customs line and showed their tickets to the clerk. As ordered, they took off their shoes and placed them in the tray. Finally, they walked through the scanner and had their bags checked.

He held her hand, and whispered, "Are you ready, my darling? Nothing but the best for you!"

"Yes, dear." He gave her a kiss, and they got on their flight. He brought his laptop so he could keep up on the other sites on the internet. They found their seats and buckled up. The plane was ready to take off. The stewardess told them what to do in an emergency.

All Glenda could think of was that this was not real. William looked at her. He said, "I made the right choice this time, Glenda."

He held her hand and gave her a kiss. The plane started flying off the ground. Within the hour, Glenda fell asleep. William (Ricardo) looked at Glenda. He shook his head. "After all I have done to you. After all the times I lied to you, you still forgive me and love me. Your love is unconditional."

He kissed her forehead. She smiled. "Maybe it was you all along I was meant to be with."

He thought of Marta. He thought about how the boss might be right about her. He needed someone that would not con you. "There are things I don't like about this job. Things I have to do you may not agree with. There will be traveling at times. Just think of it like I am protecting our family from danger."

"I don't understand. What are you going to have to do?"

"Just trust me, Glenda. It is better if you don't know. But just trust me." "You are my husband, and I will trust you."
"Glenda, I might need some help at times. Do you think you can help me?" "I will do what I can." He gave her a kiss.
"As long as you love me, everything will work out." "Then," said Ricardo, "it will work out."
He leaned over and kissed her. "I have to do some computer work this afternoon. Here is $200.00, so you can go shopping."

She asked, "Can I help with any of your computer work? I am pretty good with the computer."

"No, Glenda that is part of the work I told you that you needed to trust me. Do you think you can do that?"

"Yes, dear. I will trust you."

"Good. You are everything I hoped for. I should have married you long ago." He held her and led her to their love nest. Glenda felt loved and cherished. Ricardo realized that she was the perfect woman for him. He could do his job, and she would still love him unconditionally.

Chapter 20

Marta met Vladimir at the airport. Marta was worried and upset. She was in tears.

"What's wrong, Marta?"

"Ricardo is missing. The boss's men took him. I have no idea whether he is alive or dead."

Vladimir held her. "Don't worry, Marta. We will find him. What happened?"

Marta told the story of the boat chase. She talked about the man on the Jet Ski and how Ricardo was caught. She told Vladimir that she was not able to rescue him. Marta was afraid that the boss had gotten his revenge. She did not know what to do.

Vladimir said, "I will have my agents to find him. He is hiding somewhere. He couldn't have gone far."

Marta said, "I don't understand. Everything seemed good with us. Then he started getting depressed. We started arguing. We had never argued. I was so afraid for him. I was afraid he would be spotted and killed. I did this to him."

Vladimir calmly answered, "Ricardo is not one to stay undercover. It is the thrill of the chase and adventure that makes his life worth living. Playing it safe seems boring to someone like him."

"What about you, Vladimir?"

"There is only one woman that I want. So far, she's taken." His cellphone started ringing.

He picked up the phone. "Hello, who is this? He's where? Who is he with? What? I don't believe it!"

Marta asked, "Who is it? What happened?"

Vladimir explained that he just talked to Marcello, his lookout person, who told him that he saw someone that looked like Ricardo.

"Guess where? In Italy! He was with a girl. What's more, he had a ring on his finger."

Marta had to sit down. "This is too much, Vladimir."

Vladimir said, "Think of it this way. You have seen the rest, and now you have the best."

"Who is that, Vladimir?"

"Well, me, of course!" said Vladimir.

"I have always loved you, Marta. You never gave me the time of day. But I still loved you."

Marta replied, "Vladimir, you know it is hard having a relationship with someone in our line of work."

"Then, we don't have to let them know." He gave Marta a kiss. Marta said, "Give me some time, Vladimir."
"All right, but when you need someone to love you, I'm here."
"Thank you. I will remember that." She gave him a hug. "Now, what do we do about Ricardo?"
"We let him lead us to the boss. We track his moves over the internet. We will find the boss."

Marta replied, "I am ready to get back to work. Let's go home!"

Vladimir called the airline. Marta packed her bags. She gave a hug to her friend Nadine. Vladimir and Marta drove to the airport and checked in at the ticket counter.

"Do you have anything to declare?" asked the airport customer service representative.

"No." He took her bags and put them on the conveyor belt. He gave her a ticket. Vladimir showed his ticket to the customer service representative at the counter. He put his bags on the conveyor belt.

They decided to stop and get a cool drink before they got ready for their flight. Marta was quiet. She couldn't help thinking about Ricardo and what they had together. She was sad about the last fight they had and that she had gotten him captured. She blamed herself for things not working out.

Vladimir said, "Come on. You need to stop being so hard on yourself. The love he had for you was toxic. It was like poison. You thought you would be happy with him. He drained and changed you. You stopped playing your music. You were never happy. He is like poison. He takes you and uses you. He is not a good person to be around. You knew when you first signed up that he was no good for you. Yet, you let yourself fall in love with him. He was part of the assignment. He was not supposed to be a husband to you."

Marta replied, "I know. But he treated me so nice. He made me feel beautiful and special. He was exciting and sexy. He played the guitar. He was everything I hoped for and more."

"But Marta, he wasn't real. He was everything you wanted him to be. He became that for you. That wasn't who he was. You had to find out sooner or later."

"I know, but he is back to doing the same job for the same type of boss."

"Marta, did you really think you could change him and make him be what you wanted?"

"Yes, I did!" Vladimir.

"I believed I could get him to fight for our side. I believed that he was happy not working for the boss."

Vladimir said, "Marta, I have loved you as you are. Even when you did not love me, I loved you. I see you as you are, and I love you."

They walked into the plane and put their baggage up above their heads. They sat down. Vladimir said, "When this is all said and done, I want a chance with you."

Marta replied, "All right, when all of this is said and done."

Marta lay on Vladimir's shoulder. The plane started gearing up and then began to move off the ground. Vladimir turned on the movie monitor in front of him and plugged in his earphones. He started watching the news. Marta started dreaming about Ricardo and how she felt when he had walked and listened to her songs. She remembered dancing with him.

She remembered when he sang for her. She remembered how much he seemed to love her. Then she remembered how he changed when he became William Monroe instead of himself.

She cried to herself. "Oh, Ricardo, I miss you. Why did you choose her?"

Marta realized that they would never have a real life. There would always be conflict. However, she missed the moments and the love they shared. The flight was a little turbulent as they started flying higher. The captain reported where they were flying.

He said, "Once they get through this patch of fog they should have clear sailing." Marta tried to rest. Marta asked for a diet coke. Vladimir asked for a ginger ale.
The stewardess handed Vladimir a drink. Then she handed the coke to Marta. She turned out the light above her head and started reading.

Chapter 21

Glenda went shopping. Ricardo got on the internet and started contacting the other women to send him money. They were glad to hear from him. He gave them the information to send the money. Each believed she was the only one in his life. Each believed in a lifetime of romance. The boss contacted him by phone. He had another job for him. He was to kill Vladimir.

Ricardo never liked Vladimir. He did not like the way he drugged him and made him wake up with a new face. He didn't like that he came between him and Marta. Ricardo took the assignment. He called Glenda and told her he had to go on a short trip. The boss wired him some money.

He got a ticket at the airline counter. He was determined to get rid of Vladimir. That would make the boss know he could be trusted. Glenda would understand. She would go along with him with no questions. He caught a flight and waited for the opportunity to catch Vladimir. "Let him see what it is like to get caught.
Let him be the one that I do surgery on."

He started thinking how he was going to catch Vladimir and kill him. He devised a plan to distract him and to get him off by himself. He thought of how Marta had deceived him. He missed her and knew he could not trust her. She was not rich. She did not have an aunt. He wondered what else she had lied about. He was glad that he was with Glenda. After this assignment, they could have a normal life.

Vladimir and Marta arrived at the airport. They had had an exhausting flight. They went down to the baggage counter and waited for their luggage. After getting a rental car, Vladimir reserved two hotel rooms for them.

They picked up their baggage and headed to the hotel. After arriving, they went to their separate rooms. Marta laid her suitcases on one of the beds. She decided to take a shower and clean up. She started washing her hair, and she could hear a knock on the door. She ignored it and continued bathing. She heard a knock on the door again. She toweled off, got on her robe, and opened the door.

It was Ricardo. "Marta, I had to see you." He tried to hold her, but she turned away.

"You belong to someone else, Ricardo. You were just a coward. Instead of being with me, you are still following the boss's orders. You will never stand up to Edward!"

Marta was very angry and glared at Ricardo. Ricardo said, "I will always love you, Marta. However, I cannot change who I am. You knew that when you met me. Remember, 'You knew when we met, I'll never regret one sunrise, one sunset with you. But my journey takes a path where few ever go, so I must bid you adieu."

He gave her a hug. "Marta, I need to do something in my job that I don't want to do but have to. Please know, when it happens, I don't have a choice."

"What is it, Ricardo?"

"You don't need to know. All you need to know is when it happens, you were warned about it."

"That doesn't tell me anything! What is wrong? What are you going to do?" He smiled at Marta.

"You will find out soon enough." He kissed her and said goodbye.

Vladimir started getting ready to meet Marta in the lounge. He walked to the elevator, got in, and pressed the buttons to go up to the lounge. He had heard there was a nice view of the skylights from the lounge. He met Marta in the lounge.

She was lovely as usual. They found a table and sat down. They started looking at the city from their table by the window. Vladimir ordered two glasses of wine. Marta said, "Vladimir, I got a visitor when I went to the hotel room. It was Ricardo."

Vladimir said, "Why didn't you stop him?"

"He said that he had a job I would not like. The love pains started hitting me again. I couldn't hurt him."

"Why didn't you call me? I would have hurt him!" "That's exactly why I didn't call you Vladimir."
Vladimir said that Ricardo needed to be stopped. If he was going to do something, someone was going to get hurt.

Just then, Vladimir saw Ricardo getting out of the elevator. "I am going to end this once and for all!"

He cornered Ricardo and said, "It is over."

Ricardo said, "You are right. It's over. Hope you said your prayers, Vladimir. You are a dead man!"

Vladimir walked backward as Ricardo was pointing a gun at his head. He started pulling the trigger to shoot. At the same moment, Ricardo felt a stray bullet hitting his chest. It was from Marta.

"You married someone else after you said you loved me! All this time, you loved someone else. I am not going to let you hurt anyone else, Ricardo."

Ricardo looked at Marta in horror. "Marta, you shot me!"

Ricardo cried as he fell to the ground. Vladimir said, "Marta, what are you doing? I could have handled this!"

"I know. This was for me and for whoever else he hurt." The police heard the gunfire and came running. Marta said it was self-defense. He was trying to kill them. The police brought Marta and Vladimir in for questioning.

They called an ambulance and took Ricardo to the hospital. He had lost a lot of blood and was unconscious.

"Who is he?" asked the police.

"He is Ricardo, alias William Monroe. He was trying to kill Vladimir! I couldn't let that happen!"

Vladimir told his side of the story. He told about the boss that wanted him killed. Marta told the story of her and Ricardo. She told about how they were trying to find out information about the boss and failed. She told about how he had married someone else.

"Who did he marry?" the police inquired.

"He married someone that he had conned on the internet," Marta replied.

"This woman still wanted him and was willing to marry him." She knew he was doing jobs for the boss.

"Her name was Glenda." Glenda was called and flew to his side. She lay over his bed at the hospital and prayed for him to recover.

She cried, "I knew all along that he was doing bad things. I still loved him and wanted him as my own."

"I understand," said Marta.

"It was not that long ago I was singing songs for him about how I longed for his love and his touch. Nothing feels as good and intoxicating as his love. Nothing makes you feel so alive and so carefree. I wish that life was more like that. He is every woman's dream. Yet, he is also your nightmare when you realize how he is using you to get what he wants.

He is so good at it." Marta shook her head. "I thought I had everything figured out."
She imagined a life together, a home, and a family. "All he wanted was the next thrill, adventure, and the next job. Glenda, we were both deceived." "I was not deceived. I knew who and what he was," said Glenda.

"I still wanted him. The few moments we had together were the best days of my life."

She sobbed into her hands and cried over his bedside.

Prelude- Flaming Embers of Internet Passion By Kathy Lou When the flame of desire ignites the vibrations of your body. When tension rises and the embers grow in colors of red, orange, violet-blue, and gold, and when all you can feel you want to do is fulfill your desire, that is the flames of toxic love. It is love that can only be satisfied in the warmth of his arms. It is the longing for love, for tenderness and for the passion that may never come except in the ecstasy of your wildest dreams.

A CHANCE MEETING

He promised he would meet me and that we would find a romantic rendezvous. All I had to do was send more money, and he could get out of Nigeria. One more offering, one more promise if I only believe one more time. Would I believe it?
Would I take the little money I had to give to someone over the internet I never met? What do I do to satisfy the delicious thought and desire that was in my mind and heart? Would this be the time that he would satisfy the longings in my heart? No! Said my common sense. No! Said my brain. Yes! Said my lonely aching heart. Just one more time to believe that life could be different and he would carry me over the threshold into a new life.

Where did he go when his page disappeared? The one who said he'd love me for years and years? The face and the name I thought I knew well were now gone with my money as far as I could tell. I thought he was different, I thought he was kind, that I was his and he was mine. But now he's gone, and I'm on my own, with no more money and far from home. So is the story of the internet saga, and its sorrow, for all those who believe in a false tomorrow. The summer sea, the winter wind, all is lost and lost again. The shadows fade, the characters dance, love tells a tale and is gone at a glance. The seven seas could never tell of the unrequited love she knew so well. -

C CMAJ7 EM AM G F G C CMAJ7 F DM C EM AM F G7 C

I dream of you and what we knew of summer's warm embrace of what we lost and the high cost, and what a sad, sad waste. So many things left unresolved, so many words unsaid. We slowly drifted far apart from the day when we first wed.

Now you have yours, and I have mine, I found a love that's true. He treats me better than any man I ever knew. I long to love and trust again, to feel both young and new. To sing again a summer song, better than I had with you......

Marta was caught up in his sweet smell of deception and wrapped in a scarlet veil of lies. Common sense said walk away but her heart told her that he would change. Marta reasoned that "When I become

105

what he needs, he will be different." Ricardo wanted to continue the life and patterns from his vivid and obscure past. The time had come to walk away with no words said, just the slamming of the door Love is patient and kind, it is not selfish or rude. It does not demand its own way. It rejoices when the truth comes out Ricardo, your days of truth and recognition are coming"

Chapter 22

Marta received a call from a phone number that was not recognizable and seemed mysterious. She said, "Hello," and heard the voice on the line say, "Meet me in the second old cottage, near Cades Cove in Tennessee, the cottage near the mountain streams that was built in the 1920s. It is in the town of Elkmont. The one that is still standing but is in poor condition. I need to see you. There is so much you need to know. Come alone or don't expect to see me as you did when we last embraced." The voice gave directions and a time to meet and then hung up.

Marta hung up the phone, and her body started to tremble. Marta realized that it was Ricardo, and she felt a pang of hurt in her stomach. Realizing that he might be in danger, she drove to the place of the old cottage in spite of the red flags in her mind and heart.

She drove to Elkmont Community Association, which catered to the affluent East Tennessee/Knoxville society groups in the 1920s. They could afford to attain their dreams with cost as no object. The cottages were in disrepair, but the scene around the stream and rocks were still breathtaking.

The sky was turning pitch black as there were no lights in the abandoned area, and she heard the sound of thunder. The trees made an arch around the property, as if to say, "Stay out! You are not welcome here." Marta shuddered and walked around the lake looking for the one old cottage that was standing. She heard the sound of a hard rain and looked for shelter from the raging storm. An old and squeaky door opened by itself, beckoning her in from the cold. She felt herself drawn to the open door and walked inside. The creepy feeling and the hairs standing up on her back and her arms made her feel that someone had their eyes on her. The door made a creaky and eerie sound as it opened. She looked inside the old house and saw cobwebs on the walls and doorways. She saw the floor was caving in and the bookshelves were dusty. The room was in a state of disrepair, and it was evident that no one had been there for a long time.

She walked in and could hear the sound of her shoes on the creaky boards beneath her. The door closed behind her, and she felt a chill that made the hairs on her back and her arms stand up. She had goosebumps on her arms and could feel the breath of someone behind her. She told herself she must be imagining this and how she was feeling was emotional and irrational. Too many late-night scary movies. She turned around slowly to see who or what was behind her, and her heart froze in fear.

"Who are you and what are you doing in my house?" "Who said that? Where are you?"

Marta saw an image of a man staring at her and gasped in fright. "I am looking for someone...He said he would meet me..."

The image faded, and the room was quiet and still. Marta tried to understand what she had just seen. She walked quietly through the house and found the old stairway that led to the bedrooms upstairs. She could still feel the presence of someone near her but continued to look for Ricardo. She looked into one room and closed the door apprehensively. She went to another bedroom and noticed that the door was locked. She jiggled the doorknob and was surprised to see that it opened. She cautiously walked into the room and noticed a chair moving back and forth by itself.

Marta's heart froze with fear, and her stomach felt uneasy. This was a place that she was not welcome, and she decided to turn around and get out of this haunted and spooky place. The door opened wide, so Marta cautiously went out the door, and it slammed behind her. The sound of her heart rapidly beating and her hurried footsteps was all she heard as she ran down the stairway steps.

Doors opened and closed around her, and there were noises of clanging pots and pans and the rattling of dishes in the kitchen.
"I am trapped! Is there any way out? Why would Ricardo want me to come to such a frightening place? Hasn't he done enough to hurt me and break my heart?"

Her heart pounded as thoughts of scary scenarios from movies came into her mind. The air became unusually cool and humid around her, and she was afraid of what might happen next. She walked towards the hallway and could hear the sound of footsteps running down the stairwell.

The shadowy image became a profile as it moved closer to her. She noticed that the shape and size were familiar and wondered why she was scared but drawn to the image at the same time.
The shadowy profile opened his mouth to speak and said, "Hello Marta. There is something I need to tell you that I should have told you a long time ago."

As the profile got closer, she recognized the form, and then she looked in horror, saw the face, and screamed. She fainted and passed out on the floor. When she woke up, she saw the blurry image of someone standing over her, bending down, and looking at her with concern. She opened her eyes and recognized the face of Ricardo, and she felt comforted but confused about what she had just seen.

Ricardo said, "Marta, there are things you never knew about me, and I was afraid to tell you. Have you ever wondered why the boss was so eager to keep me or why he felt I was so good at my job? I was told that my abilities are gifts but I think they are a curse because I can never lead a normal life. Certain things trigger my *'gift'* and make me become a shadow where I *'blend into things'* and no one knows I'm there. I get these flashbacks from my childhood of wanting to be anywhere else in the world and suddenly changing where no one could see me. I thought those days were over, and now they have come back to haunt me." "What happened, Ricardo?"

"Glenda is expecting our first child, and if it is a boy it will become like me. I don't want him to have the life I had."
"What are you talking about? You should be happy. Why isn't she here to help you? Why did you call me?"
"Because she must never know what fate awaits a child that has my blood in his veins? He will never feel normal, for he will always be different."

"Ricardo, she loves you. She will understand. Why are you getting me involved?"

"Because I want you to understand I had to marry Glenda. It was either marry her or the boss and his men would hurt you. They were already out for your partner."

Marta said, "Ricardo, do you realize you are in a haunted house and you are not helping the situation? You sometimes miss the obvious when it is right in front of you. See you later."

She opened the door, walked out, and walked swiftly towards the old-fashioned train stop that was towards the front of the dilapidated old house. She sat down and tried to catch her breath and keep her heart from pacing. She looked towards the house and saw shadows moving around in the hallway. The door opened, and Ricardo walked towards her with a sad, worried look. "Marta, you are the only one who would understand. You know me. Don't you know I still love you and I'm not going to let you go?"

Chapter 23

Marta opened the car door, sat down, closed the door, and put the keys in the ignition. She turned the key and heard a grinding sound. "Come on, car start up! I gotta get out of this place." She tried again, and it started.

She said, "Thank you!" to her car as the gears were put into reverse, and she backed up the car. She heard a voice yelling, "Marta, Marta come back. Don't leave me!"

Marta said, "I won't look. I will just drive away from here and never come back!"

Marta put the car into drive and drove away from what she considered "A Godforsaken place."

Her stomach felt sick and queasy, and tears dropped on her face where it was hard to see. There were trees on each side of the road that were bending towards her car in an arc pattern. The trees seemed to be beckoning her to stay as the limbs reached towards the center of the road. Every tree seemed to reach for the center and move their limbs and leaves back to its original spot.

"My eyes are playing tricks on me!"

The phone rang and went right to text mode, and the voice from the text had her mind, heart, and body shaking.

"You will never get rid of me, Marta. I will find you wherever you go." Marta said, "Note to self, change phone number as soon as possible."

She heard a familiar voice behind her on the stairway saying, "Marta it's me! Don't you know who I am?"

"Was this Ricardo? Had the house overtaken him in waiting for me? Is he a ghost too?" Marta turned around and saw the form of a shadow on the stairway.

This was the figure she saw and heard about on television when they first met. "The news reporter said, 'He is the shadow of the night."

Marta was alarmed that the shadow was moving closer and closer to her.

Marta gripped the steering wheel and focused her attention on the road as the trees swayed back and forth around her. The moon had a white haze around it to dress up the golden white beams of its glow. The sky was dark, and the moon and headlights helped light the way to find her real home. The radio played a soft and romantic tune that reminded her of the dance she and Ricardo shared.

Memories came into her mind of their first dance together and how she told herself she would never make the mistake of falling for such a man. She thought of the summer nights on the beach in California and when she first fell in love with him when he played his guitar.

The phone rang, and Marta recognized the number on the phone and knew that it was Vladimir.

"Where are you? I haven't heard from you all day. Are you alright?" Vladimir said on the other line.

Marta smiled and said, "Yes, Vladimir. I just decided to take a drive. I'll see you in the morning."

Vladimir hung up the phone. "Oh no! He is after her again. This is going to end once and for all."

"Marta, you and I have a history together. We have a special chemistry. You can't let that go any more than I can."

"Really? Well, watch this!" She got up to leave, and Ricardo stood up and held her with a strong grip on both arms.

"Ricardo, let me go! This was a mistake coming here! Why did I come to this place?"

"Good question Marta. Why did you come to see me? Do you still feel more for me than you realize? Look into my eyes Marta and say you don't love me anymore."

She looked at him, and her words lost any resemblance of logic or thought. All she felt was emotion, and she couldn't look him in the face. She felt adrenaline going through her body, and her heart felt pain and hurt.

"I can't say it Ricardo. I want to, but I can't." Tears fell down her face and she felt her face get warmer and her slender body shaking.
"Let go!" As Marta broke free of Ricardo, she wiped the warm tears from her face and walked towards her car.

Vladimir said, "When will you realize that Ricardo is playing you just like all the other women?"
"No he isn't. He loves me."

"Marta, when will you get it through your head that a man like him can't love? They only use people to get what they want."
"I'll talk to you later Vladimir. I am on my way back." "Where were you?"
"There was this home from the 1920s I wanted to see. It turned out to be inhabited by someone or something. I admit it. This was not my best decision!"
"You have got that right. This calls for a glass of wine at Maria's diner. I hear that they are having a special artist tonight."
"Ok, I'll go but I don't plan to stay long. I have had a trying day."

"I'll pick you up at 6:30 tonight, and we will relax and have some fun."

"I'll see you then. Bye!" Maria was almost home and her heart stopped pounding inside of her.
"I'll take a nap. I will feel better after a nap."

She could still hear Ricardo's words that she would not be able to get rid of him.

"Eventually you will just be a distant memory Ricardo and I will find the kind of love that I have needed and wanted for such a long time."

Chapter 24

Glenda wept softly as she thought about her love for Ricardo. She felt the baby moved and realized that his daddy would never truly love his mama. His heart would always be with Marta. She sat at her keyboard, turned it on, and played with all the passion she had to give. Ricardo walked in as she was playing a song called "*Angels and Devils*" by Dishwalla.

Ricardo stopped and listened to the melody Glenda was playing as he walked in the door. Glenda stopped playing, turned around, and noticed the sad and solemn look on his face. She tried to stop crying, but the pain was too great to keep inside.

Ricardo walked towards her and gave her a hug and a kiss. "What's wrong Glenda? Is the baby OK? Are you alright? Why are you crying?"

Glenda stood up, turned off the keyboard, and tried to smile and act like nothing was wrong. "I was worried about you. I was worried about..."

"What? What would cause my beautiful wife to be stressed or worried? You tell me who hurt you and that will be the last of him."

"Ricardo, why did you marry me? Did you ever love me? Will the baby and I ever know your love?" Ricardo gave Glenda a look of shock, surprise, and contempt.

"Glenda, what do you mean? You know that I love you. Your emotions are getting the better of you. I noticed that you are not yourself lately. Maybe you should see a counselor. Maybe you just have some emotional problems from sometime in the past. You know I love you. I show you all the time. Don't I provide for you? Spend money on you? Why isn't that enough? It is never enough!" Ricardo gave Glenda a look of scorn, and Glenda was suddenly afraid and not knowing what to say.

Glenda said, "Ricardo, I wasn't trying to hurt your feelings. I'm sorry. It must be me. You are the perfect husband."

She gave him a kiss and a hug. "Welcome home! I have missed you!" "Glenda, I have missed you too. Let's go out, and I can celebrate my beautiful wife and the baby inside her. I heard that there is a new musician at Maria's Cafe. Why don't you put on your prettiest outfit and we'll go?"

"Alright Ricardo. You are right. That's just what I need to get out of this house." Glenda got in the shower and started singing. Ricardo smirked to himself. *Imagine Glenda thinking she is smart enough to read my mind,* he exclaimed inside his mind.

Ricardo stopped and listened to the melody Glenda was playing as he walked in the door. Glenda stopped playing, turned around, and noticed the sad and solemn look on his face. She tried to stop crying, but the pain was too great to keep inside.

Glenda stepped into the shower and felt the warm water touch her pregnant body. She could feel the baby move and started to sing the melody of the song she was playing. "*This is the last time...*" The words choked in her throat as she sang, and she started washing her long golden blonde hair. "*I wish he loved me because of me. Not because of my money and not because he has to be with me.*"

Glenda thought back to when Ricardo was in the hospital and was recovering from the bullet from when Marta shot him.

"I stayed at his side the whole time when he was recovering. In his sleep, he still called for Marta." She softly wept and put some bath salts on her scrubbie and washed herself. She sang "*La la la la lahh*" to the tune of the Angels and Demons song that was played on the keyboard.

Ricardo walked into the bedroom and could hear her singing a sad and eerie song. He walked into the bathroom and could see steam on the shower walls, and could smell the sweet scent of jasmine. Memories of being in a Turkish bath surrounded by beautiful women came into his mind. He listened to the tune and felt sad and guilty for using such a sweet girl for her money and image.

"Glenda, why did you marry me? You could have had anyone. I am sorry I hurt you. Can you ever forgive me?" He said almost as a whisper.

Glenda opened the shower door, and Ricardo could see the steam around Glenda and was amazed how beautiful she looked bearing his child.

Glenda asked, "What did you say? I didn't hear you." "I said I love you and I am a lucky man to have you."

He gave her a kiss and pulled her close to him. Glenda's heart melted with his passionate kisses. He took off his clothes and got in the shower with her and kissed her gently on the neck, cheeks, ears, and on her lips.

She felt a tingle of passion and desire. "Glenda, I need you. I don't deserve you, but I need you. Please don't stop loving me."

"I have loved you since your first internet message to me, and I have loved you more each day." She fell into his arms and felt the steam of the shower and the fire of his passion. Glenda held Ricardo close to her and she massaged his shoulders and back. She looked in his face and kissed him passionately. "Ricardo, I have missed you. When will you be able to settle down and not be traveling so much? I want our baby to know his daddy."

"Are you sure that it's a boy? Is that what the doctor said? A girl that looks just like you would be fine too. I would just have to get a baseball bat to fight off the young men that would be after her. Especially if she has your beautiful blue eyes and blond hair."

"Oh Ricardo! You are such a flatterer! But you make me so happy!" Ricardo kissed her passionately and held her close.

"Somehow Glenda," Ricardo paused and said, "We will get through this time. You were there for me in the hospital, and I will be there for you and our baby."

Ricardo washed his face and body and dried himself off. "We don't have to see the singer. I can think of something that might occupy our time."

Glenda got out of the shower and dried off. She wrapped the towel around her pregnant form and walked into the bedroom. Ricardo looked at Glenda with desire and fascination. "Let me see you just as you are."

Glenda dropped the towel, and Ricardo gave Glenda a look of delight. "That is the most beautiful thing I have ever seen in my life. You are so beautiful and you are mine. No man can ever have you but me."

Ricardo reached out to her on the bed and she fell into his arms. He kissed her softly and she felt the warmth of his charms. Glenda thought, "*He may still have something for Marta, but tonight I get to be a part of Ricardo in a way Marta could never dream of. I have someone she can never have.*"

Ricardo could tell she was thinking and asked "What's on your mind?"

"Oh, it's just the fact that I can make love to the sexiest man in the world and wake up to him. I have always loved you!"
"Then show me!"

He wrapped himself around her and she could feel all the love her husband had to give. Glenda said to herself, "*Let me tell them at the restaurant what a loving husband I have. All the women will be jealous.*" Ricardo held her close in his strong and masculine arms and showed her just how much love and passion a man could give to his woman. They snuggled in each other's arms and Glenda felt loved and desired.

Glenda said to herself, "*Yes, Ricardo is like a roller coaster that starts out slow but gives his woman a wild ride.*"

"Ricardo, I wonder if there is any other woman that is as happy as I am tonight."

"They might be happy Glenda, but you look beautiful in love." Glenda lay on Ricardo's chest and held him as she sang another love song to him.

Chapter 25

Ricardo shaved, put on some cologne, and started getting dressed. He wore a polo shirt, trousers, and his favorite silk socks with expensive Italian brown leather shoes. He combed his hair and finished getting ready.

Glenda talked from another room and said, "Ricardo, could you leave your phone at home so we won't be interrupted and have a good time?"

"Tonight I'm all yours, Glenda. Whatever you want. Where are you?" Glenda came out in her Royal Blue cocktail dress and comfortable Italian pumps. Her makeup was beautiful, and she had the confidence of a princess.
"I am right here darling! I'm ready!"

"I'll leave the phone on the front table. Let's go!" Ricardo put his arm around Glenda, opened the door, locked the door, and walked towards the car. Ricardo opened her car door and waited till she sat down and put her seat belt on.

Glenda watched as Ricardo opened his door, sat down, put on his seat belts, and put the keys in the ignition. "Glenda, you are so beautiful. I am going to make this a night to remember."

"Ricardo, you already have. I will always remember the love and desire you showed me." Ricardo put the car in reverse, backed up, and started driving towards the Bistro.

"I wonder who is playing tonight. Do you think we will see people that we know?" Ricardo's thoughts went to Marta.

"That is a possibility but the only one I will notice is you." The phone rang on the front counter as an urgent message. Since there was no one there to answer it, the message was left in text form on Ricardo's phone.

The answering machine left its message to an empty home, and Ricardo was oblivious to the seriousness of the message and the part he would have to play in the caller's scenario.

Ricardo and Glenda drove to the Bistro, and Ricardo parked the car. He opened the door for Glenda and held her hand as she got out of the car. They walked arm in arm, and Ricardo told the hostess who he was and the time of his reservation.

He found a romantic spot with candlelight and a good view of the stage. Glenda asked how his work was going and if there was anything he could tell her about his work. "Well, the boss is still looking for his wife. She left months ago and she hasn't been seen since. The police had questioned him about his wife Katie, and he said he never laid a hand on her. That she was lying. "Glenda asked, "Was she lying? Is there a reason she ran from him?"

"He finds ways to get what he wants and knows who is loyal to him and who he needs to..."

"What?"

"Never mind. You don't want to know."

"As long as he doesn't hurt you. That's what you need to understand. He can't hurt me. I have been hurt enough for one lifetime. Nothing can hurt me anymore." Ricardo's thoughts went back to the 1980s when he was eight years old, thoughts of the explosion at the nuclear plant, and him crying as he was looking for his mother in the midst of the fumes, smoke, and toxins in the air. That's when the "accident" happened.

Glenda could tell Ricardo was far away in his thoughts. She put her hand on his and said, "I love you Ricardo. We'll get through this."

Lovingly she leaned over and kissed his lips, sat down, and asked, "Is everything alright? Anything I can do?"
"Just love me Glenda and don't give up on us no matter what happens."

"Why would I give up on you?" The waiter asked what Ricardo and Glenda wanted to drink.

Ricardo said, "Cabernet."

"I'll take some water and an iced tea with lemon," said Glenda. The waiter walked away, and Ricardo looked around at the other tables as if he were lost in thought. Marta was sitting at a corner table with Vladimir, but she did not see him. Ricardo was relieved because he did not want to deal with drama tonight.

The singer and his band got up on the stage and set up their equipment. Roger Montana, the singer, was introduced by one of the band members. Roger started playing a slow tempo jazz song on the keyboard with the accompaniment of a saxophone player, guitarist, and a drummer. The song was haunting, sultry, and alluring. Ricardo asked himself, "Why do I know that song? Why is it so familiar?"

His mind flashed back to the music that was playing before the accident, and he trembled when he remembered all the words he heard that night. Ricardo said to himself, "I can't listen to this."

He asked Glenda if she would mind if he went outside to get a breath of fresh air. The waiter brought Glenda her water and iced tea, but she was oblivious to when the drinks were served.

"Have I done something wrong? Is there something I should have done?"

Ricardo is holding something inside he will not tell her about. She asked the waiter where the restrooms were, and he pointed to the lounge area.

Glenda walked towards the restroom and noticed Marta sitting with Vladimir and looking at a menu. "Now I get it. He came here to look for Marta! I should have known!"

She walked past Marta and gave her a smug look and walked towards the lounge. Marta thought, "Was that Glenda? Does not mean Ricardo is here? Oh no! He is the last person I want to see tonight."

She signaled the waiter and requested a glass of Chablis. Vladimir said, "I'll have a rum and coke."

The waiter walked away with their drink orders. "Vladimir, maybe I should say something to Glenda to let her know that I am not a threat. What do you think?"

"You need to stay out of their relationship. Let Ricardo deal with his wife. You don't need to be involved."

Marta said, "Vladimir, let's dance! You said we would have fun tonight."

Vladimir scooted out Marta's seat and took her by the hand and led her to the dance floor. . Ricardo walked back into the restaurant, sat down, and started drinking his wine.

Glenda came back to the table and asked Ricardo, "Did you know that she was here? Did you plan this?"

"What are you talking about? You know! Marta is here." "No! I told you I was here for you. I didn't know she would be here." "Are you telling me the truth?"

"Yes! Let's get up and dance and show what a happy married couple we are." Ricardo led Glenda to the dance floor and danced to a slow and melancholy song.

Chapter 26

"Ricardo?" "Yes, Glenda."

"How did you learn to play the guitar?" Ricardo's face looked solemn and retrospective as he paused and started dancing again.

"All I had left of my dad was his old guitar and I wanted to play it. I thought that if I learned to play on his guitar that I could feel close to him again. My boss found the best teachers for me and I learned Blues guitar, Spanish guitar, and some flat picking. He said, 'Only the best for you,' and I was an eager student.

Music was the one thing that made sense and it helped me when I remembered things that I wanted desperately to forget."

"Like what? Ricardo! Please let me into your world. What happened that keeps you up at night? What is tormenting you?"

"Glenda, I don't want to talk about it. Let's just enjoy this dance and maybe I can get the band to play our song."

Glenda put her arms around him and said, "Ricardo, no matter what happened, no matter what you have done I will still love you."

"I know Glenda, but some things are better when they are left buried in the past."

Vladimir watched Ricardo and Glenda dancing and remarked, "They are an attractive-looking couple! That Glenda looks like she's ready to pop! I wonder if she is having twins."

Marta could tell that she was supposed to give some sort of reaction but at this point, she just wanted Vladimir to shut up about Ricardo so she could pretend he wasn't there and enjoy the music.

"Vladimir, do me a favor." "Anything for you Marta."

"Kiss me! Kiss me passionately and desperately like I was the only woman you had ever seen or wanted. Hold me with all the passion you have got and kiss me. Wash Ricardo and his memory out of my mind." Vladimir looked at Marta with longing and desire and got up from his chair.

He walked to her side of the table, took her hand and helped her get up. He looked into her beautiful brown eyes and said, "All you had to do was ask."

Marta could feel his warm and tender lips against hers as he held her close to his body. Desire flooded through her like a bubbling fountain. Marta attempted to recover from Vladimir's passionate kiss and felt the flames of desire come over her once again.

"Vladimir, I didn't know you could kiss like that."

Vladimir gave Marta a serious look and said, "You have got to understand something about me. I will never come second to any man. I have always loved you. Somehow you have got to make the choice that it's either me or him."

"Marta, do you remember when you first decided to join the FBI and why this field was important to you?"
Marta sipped on her wine and pretended to look away. "Well, do you remember?"

Marta looked down at the table and could feel her emotions taking control. "Vladimir that was a long time ago. He has been dead for several years. I still can't talk about it without remembering."

Vladimir paused and decided to speak to her in a more sympathetic tone. "Marta, I know that he was important to you and no one should have had to experience losing someone at such a tender age."

Marta had trouble getting the words out and started crying. "He was just sitting there in the house and he was not hurting anybody. Why did that gang have to be shooting at houses? Why did they pick mine?"

"Remember when you joined the police force? I thought you would never make it. You were 'too soft' for this job and I knew it. I taught you how to shoot and how to defend yourself. I wanted you to see yourself as the woman you are now. Don't you know that being with Ricardo is taking you backwards in your life and career? Marta, you will never come first! There will always be another woman, another job, or something that will come up where you will come second. Is that what you want?"

Marta exclaimed, "No! That's not what I want! I want a home and a family again. I want someone to love me where I will never have to be afraid again."

Vladimir said in a loving and gentle voice, "Marta, don't you know? You are looking at him. All I ask for is a chance."

"Marta, I never gave up on you and the harder you tried to make it the more I admired you. I was surprised when you followed me to the FBI."

"I followed you but never realized what I was walking into. How do you keep the emotion out of it? My friend's dad was a police officer and I learned to keep my feelings to myself. That way you don't get hurt."

"Vladimir, sometimes you will have to let someone in and let go. Love involves vulnerability."

"If anyone has made me feel vulnerable it's you Marta. I was left with your dog while you were with another man."

"You see Vladimir, I will never stop learning from you. I never realized that I need you."

Ricardo looked at the table and gazed at Marta. "Glenda, Marta was a fantasy for me and I wanted her with everything I had but I am beginning to realize what I have right now. Listen! They are playing our song."

The musician started playing *Fields of Gold* on the guitar. Ricardo looked at Glenda and said, "He's playing our song."

Glenda was led on to the dance floor and walked through fields of gold with her lover, husband, and confidant.

Marta thought back on what her life was like before she joined the police force. "Vladimir, I know that I wasn't the easiest person to teach. I was stubborn, moody, and unsure of myself. I was used to being dependent on a man and when my son's dad left I didn't know what to do. I had to learn to take care of a son and be a dad and mom. When my son Michael wasn't a part of my life, I felt that I had lost myself. I didn't know how to go on."

Vladimir said, "I knew if anyone could succeed you could. While others were giving up, you kept trying."

Marta shook her head and gave a thoughtful look towards her plate. "Vladimir, I have learned that there are a lot of jobs one can do when they are given no other choice but to survive."

Glenda held Ricardo in her arms and said, "This is a perfect night!"

His passionate and gentle kisses were on the nape of her neck, cheeks, ears, and her tender lips. Strong and masculine arms embraced and caressed Glenda as they danced.
"You know Glenda, I am a very lucky man."

Passionate kisses were given as the music of *Fields of Gold* by Sting serenaded the two lovers.

Ricardo said, "Glenda, you had everything a person could want. I don't understand why you fell for me. I saw the people in your circle, and I know that they were warning you about me and that I was not good for you. I did not love you at the beginning, and you know I was only out for one thing, and that was your money."

Glenda looked into Ricardo's eyes and said, "Yes, you are right, Ricardo, that I had everything money could buy. All I had to do was wave money under someone's nose, and they would do anything I told them to."

"Then why?" Glenda got misty-eyed and said, "Money could not bring happiness, nor could it keep my mom and dad together.

Money cannot buy love or happiness that lasts for longer than the purchase and the price one pays for it. I didn't care if I gave it all up just to find someone who would love me and couldn't be bought. I was given an added bonus when I noticed that you were handsome, sexy, and an excellent musician."

Ricardo gave her a soft kiss and said, "I bet you say that to all the dark-haired and dark-eyed guitar players."

Glenda smiled and said, "You are the first one I met so it must be you that I admire."

Chapter 27

Marta said, "Vladimir, do you remember when I was learning target practice and I couldn't aim straight and almost shot you?" "Yeah, did you ever wonder why when you had a bow and arrow, gun, mace, or other items that I stayed to the side and let you practice?"

"Well, now you know why!!" Marta laughed and said, "You taught me how to build my confidence. I never used a gun before or had to defend myself. You taught me what to do if I was ever in a situation where I was in danger."

"I still don't understand why you joined the FBI. I never thought you would want to work as a spy."

"Vladimir, do you remember when I found the gang that did the drive-by shootings? One by one I led them to justice. I was determined they would never ruin anyone else's life. I almost took the law into my own hands, but I let the law determine their fate. I wanted to hurt them just as bad as they hurt me."

"Marta that is the difference between you and them. You have a conscience. They are just part of a gang initiation."

"Vladimir, I am not sure if having a conscience is always a good thing. You feel guilty no matter what decision you make. You don't know how I wanted to sneak into the prison and end their lives, but I knew it would make me just like them."

Ricardo and Glenda went home and walked in the door. Ricardo could hear his phone beeping and picked up his phone. There was an "urgent message" according to the text. Ricardo said to Glenda, "I wonder who called me? I guess I need to find out."

He listened to his messages, and his eyes got big, and the color drained from his face. His hands started shaking, and he dropped the phone. Ricardo stood in one place in what seemed like a catatonic state. Glenda had been in the bedroom changing her clothes and walked towards the kitchen.

Ricardo stood in one place and was gasping and holding onto the chair. Glenda rushed to his side and asked, "What's wrong? Are you OK? Ricardo, what happened?"

Ricardo stood there in silence with his mouth open and in a state of shock. "Ricardo! What happened? Do I need to get you to the hospital?"

Ricardo slowly looked at Glenda and back into space, and Glenda became worried that he was having a seizure or a heart attack. "Ricardo!"

Ricardo looked at Glenda and said, "It's my brother. It's been so many years since I saw him. I thought he was dead, but he just called me, and he's alive! He wants to see me, and he will be flying here within the next few days. I don't know what to say. The last time I saw him was when he was eight years old when we left Ukraine and went to England. Oh my... He's alive!"

Glenda asked, "Who's alive? What are you talking about?"

Ricardo put his hand on his head and put his hand on a chair to keep from falling down. "That's it! I'm calling the Dr's office. You are going to the emergency room! Ricardo, what can I get you? Do you need some water, oxygen, what can I do?"

Ricardo looked to the right, down, and grabbed the kitchen chair with both hands. "When I was little, my family and I were in a bad accident, and my brother was in poor health because of it. When I left our foster home, I thought he was dying because he was scarred from the toxins. I did not think he would survive, and I did not want to see my last family member dead because I wanted to remember my brother as he was."

"I didn't know you had a brother. Tell me about him." "He was young and a lot of fun that was before..."

"Before what?" Glenda sat down next to Ricardo and put her arm around his shoulder.

"Before he changed from the accident, and I didn't recognize him anymore. I had to leave."

Glenda spoke with compassion and tenderness, "I understand, Ricardo."

"Is this what you have been keeping inside all these years?"

I blamed myself. He was my little brother, and I should have protected him somehow."

"What kind of accident, Ricardo?" Ricardo's mind raced back to that day in 1988 when his whole world changed, and he was no longer innocent from the world's dangers. He could still remember calling his mom's name and realizing that she would not survive the toxins that had already crept into her bloodstream.

"Ricardo, we need to see him! He is your brother. We will welcome him with open arms! You mean, whatever he looks like now you will accept him? Do you realize what you are saying? Have you ever seen what toxins can do?"

"Glenda, my dad died of cancer because of the toxins in the air. He could not breathe anymore and had cancer of the esophagus." "Ricardo, he is reaching out to you. We need to be there for him."

"You are too sweet for your own good, Glenda. Make sure you keep your distance from him."

"Why?"

"You might get infected by him and it will kill the baby or make him not look human. Ricardo, please call him! Do you have his number?"

"Alright, Glenda, I will call him. Are you sure you want to walk into this?" "With all my heart, Ricardo. I am here to support you no matter what."

"I will call for your sake, but as far as I am concerned, this is a nightmare."

"Ricardo dear," Glenda said, "This might be the only way that you will finally have peace."

"Okay, okay! You win." Ricardo dialed the number and listened to the dial tone to see who or what would answer.

Ricardo tried to talk himself out of calling, but Glenda kept insisting. Ricardo wrote down the phone number from the text and dialed the number.

The phone rang two, three, four times, and Ricardo started to hang up until he heard a familiar voice with a Ukrainian and English dialect say, "Hello, Who is it?."

Ricardo's throat felt scratchy, and he felt weak in the knees.

He took a deep breath and said, "I got a call from this number. Who is this?"

Laughter could be heard on the other side of the phone and made Ricardo uncomfortable and upset.

"You mean, you really don't remember me or let's say you were trying to forget me. Take a guess, Ricardo. That is what they call you now, isn't it?"

Anger and fear welled up inside, and Ricardo said in a loud defensive tone, "This isn't funny. If this is a practical joke I will track you down. I guarantee this will be the last joke you play."

The voice said, "I am not playing a joke and I have tried for years to find you. I bet you thought I was dead didn't you? Well, surprise! I'm not! Come on Ricardo. Guess who this is."

Chapter 28

Vladimir drove Marta home and parked in her driveway. Marta asked if he would like to come in, and he eagerly accepted her invitation. Marta stepped out of the car, found her keys in her purse, and walked into the house with Vladimir.

Marta could hear an excited bark and opened her arms to a loving beautiful dachshund. "Coco Biscuit! Love you, baby girl."

Coco saw Vladimir, jumped on the couch, and barked happily.

"Hello, little girl. Have you been a good girl while your mama is gone?" "Arf arf," said Coco as she smiled and wagged her tail.

Vladimir rubbed her chin, her head, her ears, and kissed her. "Marta, Coco and I became good friends while you were in California. We spent evenings together catching up on our favorite television shows."

Marta responded sarcastically, "So that is why she runs back and forth when there is a detective show!"

Vladimir laughed and said, "I guess so. She likes catching the bad guy." Marta and Vladimir talked about what they had learned in protecting the peace and how accidents, murders, and other tragedies had changed the way they looked at life.

"Vladimir, do you remember when we first met Ricardo, and you played jealous and engaged in a sword fight with him at Maria's Bistro?"

Vladimir blushed and said, "Maybe that wasn't a good idea, but I was trying to have a bit of 'flash' to my character."

Marta remarked sarcastically, "You added flash and a bit of Errol Flynn. Luckily Maria convinced the customers that it was just part of the act. You were an actor that wanted to give a sample of the new play you were in."

"I thought I made a good Errol Flynn. Not to be outdone Vladimir said, "I was ready to take my show on the road. You never know when there might be a following for a sword fighter." "I'm sure if you play the same act, you will get a following. Not the one you want!" Vladimir and Marta laughed as they reminisced the night they started trailing Ricardo.

"You know, it's funny. He never figured out that we were trailing him or that we were agents."

Vladimir smiled at Marta and looked into her eyes. "Marta, that is because all he could see was your beauty. That's all I see right now."

Katie talked to the attorney that had been appointed to her through the State, named Jermaine Graft. He was a distinguished - looking gentleman, with gray hair at his temples, a slight beard, and was in his mid-40s. Mr. Graft had a reputation for being ruthless against corruption and distortion. Attorney Graft was appointed because of her husband's connections with the mob and the level of abuse Katie had suffered.

Katie walked into the attorney's office building, introduced herself, and waited till Attorney Graft was able to see her.

He came out to the lobby to greet her and invited her into his office. "Hello, I'm Jermaine Graft and I was appointed to your case."

Shyly Katie said, "I'm Katie. I am hoping you can help me get a protective order against my husband."

Katie smiled and said, "I know you. I mean I have never met you personally, but I know you. Your name is Marta, isn't it?"

Marta was startled but curious how the waitress would know who she was. Marta said sarcastically, "Well, you know who I am. I am definitely at a disadvantage here. What have you heard?"

Katie did not expect that response and thought for a minute. "Oh, I have only heard good things about you. How would I hear any difference?"

Marta looked at Katie with an inquiring look and said, "There's something about you and I have got a feeling that you are here because you don't want to be seen in public places."

"Believe it or not, my instincts tell me that I was supposed to talk to you."

Katie exclaimed, "I am not sure why you would say that. I am just an ordinary waitress!" Katie's hands trembled, and she was glad that nothing was in her hands. Marta looked at her as if she was cross-examining a fugitive.

"Then," she looked at Katie's name tag and said, "Katie, how did you know my name?"

Katie felt embarrassed, and her face started turning warm and feverish. "You look like someone. Maybe I was wrong. Have you decided what you would like to eat? We have some specials on the inside of the menu."

"Hmm...I'll take a chicken salad with vinaigrette dressing and some more coffee." Katie wrote down her order, took her menu, and walked towards the kitchen.

Marta spoke up and said, "One more thing, Katie." She turned around and said, "Is there something else you would like?"

"No, but there is something I want to offer you." Katie was puzzled about what Marta could offer her.

"If you ever need my help or you ever feel like you are in danger or need to talk, here is my card. All you have to do is call." Katie gratefully took Marta's card and said, "Thank you," as she took the card and walked away.

Katie glanced at the card and realized who it was and was shocked that providence had taken a hand on her behalf. The card said her name was Marta and that she was in a Special Forces unit for criminal investigations.

Katie said to herself, "I hope there will never be a time before the court hearing that I will have to call Marta. If I do, I hope that it is for a casual meeting not out of fear."

Katie had gotten the orders from others in her section and brought the orders to the chef. Katie started preparing the chicken salad for Marta and added extra vegetables and tomatoes. The salad was topped with a homemade chicken salad mixture. Katie put the salad on the plate and added Texas toast on the side. She made some vinaigrette dressing and added feta cheese to the top of the salad.

The salad was presented to Marta with a fresh cup of coffee. Marta looked up from her phone and said, "My! That is a beautiful salad. I bet you are the one that keeps this place in business!"

Katie smiled and said, "We all do our part." Katie got the other orders and served other customers in her section. Marta observed that Katie was in demand and everyone wanted to be in her section.

Marta asked herself, "I wonder who she really is. Her eyes opened wide, and she almost choked at the realization that this was 'not just anybody.' This was Edward's wife and that he would stop at nothing to find her and kill her."

Marta said to herself, "I better warn her that Edward told Ricardo that he is out for revenge and that he has been searching diligently for her.. There has got to be something I can do."

Katie went home after her evening shift and checked her phone messages. There were several messages, and Katie wondered who had her number. She pressed the four-star code for her messages and heard a familiar voice vocalizing in a tearful and angry tone, "Katie, come home! Why did you run away? You are my wife, and you know that I love you! I am not going to be made a fool of so you better come home now! I found your number and you know that if you don't come home I will find you. Katie, you know what happens when people cross me. You better think about it Katie and get over your emotional problems."

Katie hung onto the phone for several minutes and shook with fear and terror. She left a message with her attorney and then called the police. "I wonder if this is why Marta stepped into my life. Maybe she can help protect me after all?"

Chapter 29

Ricardo looked at Glenda and glanced at the phone. "Yes, I know who you are, Joey. I have not seen you in a long time."

Ricardo paused and said, "I am glad you are okay."

"Yes, Ricardo, I am okay. You would not believe what the wonders of modern science can do. I am a walking, talking, breathing '*wonder of nature*.' Believe it or not, I even have a family and a beautiful wife, and they are all healthy."

Ricardo replied in a concerned tone, "Joey, when I saw you, I thought you were not going to make it, and my boss would not let me bring you with me."

"I would not have wanted you to work for him anyway." Joey asked, "Why not?"

"Joey, he is not a good man, and you were better off being at the foster home."

"Ricardo that is where you were wrong. My parents were dead, and my brother was gone. My foster parents treated me like a son, but they could not take your place in my life." Joey paused and said in a determined tone, "I had made an oath to myself to find you and be a part of your life again."

"Ricardo, do you remember in school when you started changing? Sometimes that happens to me too, and the worst times!"

Ricardo laughed and shook his head, saying, "Yeah, tell me about it. I am changing more now, and I am not sure what to do about it."

Joey asked, "Would you like to speak to your nephews and nieces?" "Yes! Can I put it on speaker phone so Glenda can hear?"

"Of course, Ricardo."

Ricardo put the phone on speaker and said, "Hi Glenda! You finally got the playboy to settle down."

Glenda laughed and said, "I don't think Ricardo will ever settle down, but he made sure I would."

Glenda said excitedly, "Ricardo and I are having a baby!" "Well, what do you know? Congratulations to both of you!"

Joey got to thinking about what was going through his brother's mind and decided to reassure him. "Ricardo, I know that you are nervous, but don't be. Everything is going to turn out fine."

"Joey, you have always understood me, and it was not until this moment I realized how much I missed you and Mom and Dad. I tried to shut off those emotions so I would not get hurt."

Joey said sympathetically, "The only way to deal with emotions is realizing what is causing pain in your life and deal with it."

Ricardo asked Joey, "How did you find me?"

"I saw you on the news and thought that there could only be one person who would be looked on as a 'shadow.'"

Ricardo said, "When are you coming?"

"I was thinking about coming to your area in a couple of weeks." Glenda said, "You can stay with us. We would be glad to have you!" Joey said reassuringly, "We'll keep in touch. See if you can keep Ricardo in line, Glenda! Bye, Ricardo!"

"Bye, Joey!"

Ricardo hung up the phone. "Ha! Ha! Joey was always a jokester! I can't believe that I talked to him after all this time!"

Glenda gave Ricardo a hug and said, "I love you, Ricardo!"

Glenda could feel his warm lips against hers and he said softly, "I love you too!"

Katie picked up her cell phone and thought of the conversation that she had with Marta. She looked at the phone number on the card and decided to call Marta and tell her what was going on. She anxiously dialed the number and listened to the dial tone.

Marta went into the kitchen and picked up the phone. "Hello." "Who is this?"

"This is Katie. Do you remember that you said to give you a call if I felt that I might be in danger?"

Marta felt a cold chill go up her spine and realized that Edward was involved in some way. Marta paused and cautiously answered, "Yes, I remember that I told you to call if there was danger. Are you in danger, Katie?"

A picture came up on Katie's phone of the bathroom mirror with something written in dark red lipstick. She took a closer look at the phone picture and it said, "Why? I love you!"

Katie realized that Edward was trying to coax her back home. Marta said in a concerned voice, "Katie! What's wrong? Is someone there? Tell me what is going on!"

Katie could hear the sound of loud footsteps outside her beach house. Katie said in a frightened voice, "Marta, there is someone outside! I don't feel safe!"

Marta tried to remain calm and asked, "Where are you?"

In a worried tone Marta exclaimed, "Katie! How can I get to you?" Marta heard a scream and the phone went dead. "Katie! Hello! Hello!"

Katie heard someone knocking on the door. She listened to the sound, panicked, and decided to hide under her bed. She heard someone trying to force the window to open and Katie held her breath in nervous anticipation.

Her fear got the best of her, and she asked herself, "Who is trying to break in?"

She heard a knock on the door again and someone jiggling the doorknob in a determined and forceful manner. Then she heard the crash of the front door busted open and the door falling to the ground. *Where's my phone? Where did I put it?*

She grabbed her phone and attempted to dial 911 but her hands were shaking. Katie looks for a means of escape through a window or door. The sound of angry footsteps were all she could hear and her heart almost stopped when she recognized the walking pattern.

All that could be heard were the sound of footsteps along with the angry voice that had haunted her every day for the last 10 years saying, "I told you I would find you! Where are you hiding?"

She heard the sound of footsteps, the squeak of her bedroom door opening, and the sound of a man muttering in an angry tone. Footsteps were heard walking towards the closet and the door opening and closing. The bathroom door was opened and the room was walked through as if someone was looking for something or somebody.

An eerie sense of quiet filled the room and the sense of forbidding and anticipation of danger was more than Katie could bear. Her heart started beating faster and Katie wondered if her husband could sense the intense fear that was quivering up inside her.

The bottom bedspread was lifted and Katie saw eyes of fire and an evil grin as Edward said, "At last I found you. Peekaboo Katie!"

As Edward grabbed her arms, started cursing at her, and dragged her out from under the bed, Katie fell into a state of fear and terror. It was as if she was watching herself and this man as a third person.

The next thing she remembered was waking up in her bed and realizing that this was just another night that she could see the last day of her existence-when the nightmares about Edward would come true and she would never wake up again.

This time the dream was so real she could feel the bruises and the pain from his violent anger. She looked up to heaven and said, "Oh God please don't let this dream become a reality. Don't let Edward ever hurt me again."

The phone rang and Katie nervously picked it up. "Katie, this is Marsha from Attorney Jermaine Graft's office. He wanted to let you know that there is a court date set for a protective order regarding your husband Edward. It will be next Tuesday morning at 9:00 am. I need to let you know Edward might be there with his attorney to hear the verdict."

Katie shook as she held the phone to her ear. "I understand. Then I can be safe, right? Once the order is signed he can't hurt you or even come near you or he will be put in jail."

"Tuesday it is then." "Thank you!" "Have a good day Katie."
Katie hung up the phone and looked up to heaven. "Thank God it will be over soon."

Ricardo got a call from Edward and was hesitant to pick it up. He walked to the phone and said, "Hello."
Edward sarcastically said, "How nice it is to pick up your phone. I have a job for you."

Ricardo listened to Edward and shook his head as he intently listened to Edward's instructions.

"OK. I will do it." Ricardo started packing and Glenda asked where he was going.

Ricardo said, "Its business. I will be back before my brother comes. Hold down the fort, Glenda."

"Do I have a choice?"

Ricardo laughed, "Yes you do but I am glad you are making the choice to stay with me."

Edward wanted Ricardo to pull a bank heist and use his skills to appear invisible. Edward needed money because of the high attorney fees he was having to pay.

Ricardo was told what bank to go to and what time it was not busy. With careful planning, he calculated the day and the time for the heist.

The next day, Ricardo walked into the bank as if he was a customer and his "special gift" helped him to fade into the scenery.

He became invisible and walked past the guards, the tellers, and after careful speculation, found out where the bank vault was. Now it was time for a distraction, where people could focus on something else, while he was figuring out the vault combination.

He lit a match and threw it inside a nearby trash can and trash and papers caught on fire. The smoke alarm went off, the sprinklers went off in the building, and Ricardo carefully figured out the combination and walked into the vault without being observed.

Ricardo walked into the vault but no one could see who was opening the door or what was happening. The bank manager tried to close the vault but got "knocked out" and hit the floor.

Shots could be heard as bags of money seemed to be suspended in midair and going off by themselves. One of the tellers exclaimed, "It's the shadow like on TV. There must be a way to catch him."

Ricardo put on a dark trench-coat and a hat so he could not be recognized and hid the bags of money in his large coat as he walked out of the bank into his getaway car. Marta turned on the news and the headline story was about the shadow again.

Marta laughed and said, "Let me see where I have heard this story before? It must be Ricardo up to no good!"

Vladimir called after the news story and Marta knew exactly what he was calling about. "Did you hear about?"

"Yes, Vladimir it's Ricardo again. It's like being in an old time melodrama." "No one will believe it was Ricardo. They were not able to see him."

"I wonder what he needed the money for." Marta started thinking about Katie and realized that Ricardo was getting money for Edward and that Ricardo did not have a choice.

Edward would make him take the blame and deny he ever asked Ricardo to steal for him."

Vladimir said sternly, "You need to find Katie and keep her out of danger before the hearing."

All the news stations were talking about the bank vault opening by itself and money walking off by itself in bags. They caught the form of a shadow but it was hard to pin down and then the shadow disappeared.

The headlines read, "Shadow at large! There were scenes from Orson Welles in "The Shadow Knows."

There were rewards for whoever could catch the shadow. Marta turned off the television and said, "Ha! I wonder what Ricardo is worth?"

"$1,000.00? Maybe more?" In the meantime, Ricardo brought the money to Edward.

Edward said, "One more thing Ricardo. I want you to lead me to where Katie is hiding. We will go tonight and pick something up to eat at the beach. I heard that there is a good restaurant close to the Riverside condos."

Chapter 30

Edward's driver drove Edward and Ricardo towards the beach.

Edward looked at Ricardo and said, "You know, Katie and I met at the beach. I was playing beach volleyball. I thought she was the most beautiful woman I had ever seen. I don't understand, why would she run from me? I took care of her and made sure the bills were paid. You know sometimes you have to keep a woman in line and make sure she does what you expect her to. But everyone knew I loved her. Why didn't she know? I said I was sorry when I got angry at her. Why couldn't she ever forgive me? I even got on my knees and asked her to forgive me after I became enraged with her and knocked her down. My friends and my girlfriends forgive me because I am such a nice guy. Everybody loves me but her. I don't understand it. "Ricardo shook his head, "Yeah, I don't understand women either."

The breeze was cool and crisp from the ocean, and Ricardo could feel that there was something about this area. He felt a sense of foreboding like something might happen on this restless, disturbing night, and he wanted to go back home to be with his wife and baby.

Katie went outside of the shop to get some air and saw the form of Edward's car driving into the parking lot. Suddenly, a feeling of nausea and fear mixed with adrenaline filled her body, and she felt weak at the knees.

She saw Edward and Ricardo walk in, and another waitress greeted them, putting two menus on the table. Katie told the chef, "I need to go."

"You can go after you finish waiting on your tables."

Katie tried to think of a clever disguise but couldn't figure out what she should do. She brought a cup of coffee to one of her tables and tried to keep her head down so Edward would not recognize her. Ricardo turned around to find a waitress and noticed a familiar form and face. He smiled at her, and Katie put her finger to her mouth so Ricardo would not say anything. Ricardo excused himself and told Edward he would be back as he headed towards the restroom.

He spotted Katie and warmly said, "It's been a long time." "Yes Ricardo, it has been. Please don't give me away."

"Katie, he doesn't know you are here. I can't protect you. You are going to have to be strong."

Katie turned around and noticed that Edward was looking in the direction that Ricardo was and wondered who he was talking to. Edward asked Ricardo, "Who is it?"

Edward recognized the slim waist and the pretty physique of the waitress. When Ricardo turned around, Edward realized that it was his wife and that she had been at this diner all along.

He said, "Hello Katie. It's been a long time."

Katie froze in fear and dropped the coffee pot, leaving all the pieces of the glass and coffee spread out on the floor. Katie started panicking and found a mop and bucket to clean up the coffee. She swept up the broken glass off the floor.

Edward said, "Katie, why don't you understand I can't let you go and that you are mine? Now that I have found you I am not letting you out of my sight. Tonight you are coming home and we can start again."

Katie woke up in a cold sweat. The nightmares are happening again. "When will I stop being afraid of Edward? When will I feel that he won't hurt me anymore?"

Tears filled her eyes, and she could still feel the fear and anxiety from the dream. She got up and made a cup of coffee to calm her nerves. "It is going to be alright. I will get protected custody, and it will be alright."

There was a knock on the door, and Katie shivered with terror and trepidation at the thought of seeing Edward again. One knock, two, three. The doorbell started ringing, and then there was a knock on the window. Did she dare to look out? Would this be the last sound she would hear?

Katie walked to the door and shyly said, "Who is it?"

The landlord said, "There is a letter that was forwarded to you and it ended up in my post box. It looks like it has been traveling for a while."

Katie cautiously put out her hand for the letter and thanked the landlord. She closed the door, sat on the couch, and opened the letter slowly and carefully.

She took a deep breath and noticed the quick cursive handwriting that could have only come from... Edward... She opened the folds of the letter and stared at the words, and a cold chill went up and down her back.

She fell to her knees and said, "No! No! Don't do it Eddie! Please God no!" Katie held the letter in her shaking hands and trembled as she read the words.

"Dear Katie, you were wrong in leaving me and you should know by now that I get angry and I don't mean what I say.

Please come back to me because I cannot live without you. I will do whatever I can to get you to come back. I am sure that you don't want any of your family hurt by your decision. For their sake I suggest you come back now and end this foolishness of leaving me.

If they get hurt or something of yours gets broken, realize just whose fault it is and that you brought it on. I will start with your brother.

Yours, Edward."

Katie called Marta and asked if she could meet her at the diner. She told her about the letter from Edward and was worried what he would do next. Marta met her at the diner after work and looked at the letter. "As far as I know he is bluffing, but you need to show this letter to the police and talk to your attorney about having your court date sooner to have a restraining order put in place. This is for your protection."

"I will. Worst case scenario, could I stay with you?"

Marta gave some thought to Katie's question. "Yes, you can stay with me but realize that I am not home all the time. The restraining order needs to be put in place first."

"Agreed," said Katie.

"He wouldn't really hurt my family would he?"

Katie nervously picked up her cellphone and called her mother. "Hello? Is that you Katie? Are you alright? Edward called and said he wanted to come over and tell us some bad news about you." Katie exclaimed, "He called? You are not going to have him over are you?"

Her mother said, "Well Katie, we didn't know what to think. No one has heard from you in months. Edward is on his way over and he is taking Tommy (Katie's brother) on a fishing trip.

"Mom," Katie paused and said, "whatever you do don't let Edward in that door. I am saying this for your safety."

Helen, Katie's mother said, "But Katie, he was just trying to be helpful. Are you afraid he might do something to our family? Are you afraid he will hurt Tommy? What is going on?"

"I will explain it later. Call the police! Don't let him in!" Helen looked through the curtain window and saw a black sedan pulling up into the driveway.

Katie said, "It's too late. He is driving up to the house."

A car door opened and slammed shut and there was a pair of black patented shoes walking from the driveway to the door.

"Katie, what do you want me to do?" Katie spoke in a shaken but firm tone, "Mom, call the police now!"

Helen hung up the phone and started calling the police. Tommy said, "Is that Edward? I'll get it!"

Helen exclaimed in a frightened tone, "No Tommy! It's not the person you think it is. For God's sake, don't open the door."

Chapter 31

The doorbell made a loud and piercing sound, and Helen was afraid to open the door. A series of knocks were heard on the door and the window. Helen looked out the window and saw Edward walking around the house as if he was looking for something. The phone rang one, two, three times as Helen tried to gain her composure and figure out things to protect themselves.

Tommy was puzzled why his mom was not answering the door and saw his mom shaking and trembling and holding her heart. "Mom, do I need to call the doctor? Are you having a heart attack?"

"No, Tommy. But we need to call the police because Edward is bad news."

Tommy grinned and said in a reassuring manner, "He's not so bad. He just has a temper."

"Do you realize who he is or what he could do?"

The doorbell rang, and Tommy opened the door. Edward looked impatient as he looked at Tommy's face.

"What took so long? I was getting worried about you. Are you ready to go?"

Tommy looked at the helpless face of his mother. "Mom, will you be ok? We will just be gone for a few hours."

Edward looked at Helen and asked what was wrong. Helen exclaimed, "I am worried about my daughter. Are you two ok?"

"Of course! She knows Tommy and I are going fishing. She is all for it!" Edward motioned for Tommy to get his gear and head out the door.

"Edward, you wouldn't ever hurt Tommy, would you?" Edward smiled and told Tommy, "It was time to go."

Tommy looked sadly at his mom and said, "Don't worry, mom. Edward will take care of me."

"Helen, I will take care of him. You know I will!" "Edward that is what I'm afraid of."
Edward snickered and said, "See you later!"

Tommy and Edward walked towards the car, got in, and drove away. Helen had a sinking feeling in her stomach and sat down.

Tommy smirked, "I can't understand my mom! She is so melodramatic!" Edward said, "Why do you say that? She just cares about you!"

Tommy shook his head and said, "I'm not a kid anymore. She needs to stop worrying about me."

"Well," Edward muttered, "Whether you should worry depends on your sister and how devoted she is to her family."

Tommy heard Edward mutter but couldn't understand him. "Huh? What did you say? Did you say something about my sister?"

Edward spoke in a consoling tone. "No, I didn't say anything. You want to get some pizza first? I know a great pizza place. its a few blocks away."

"Oh, you are talking about the 'Mellow Mushroom.' That is my favorite pizza hangout."

"Good. I'm getting kind of hungry." Edward drove into the parking lot and parked the car.

"Guess what! Pizza is on me!"

"Thanks, Edward. I never turn down pizza."

"A true teenager after my own heart. How old are you now?" "I just turned 15. I am going to be driving soon."

Edward smiled, looked up from his menu, and said, "Yeah, that's right, Tommy."

"You might even work for me someday." "Really, Edward?" "Tommy, you would not believe what you will get to do with me at the wheel. Come on! Pizza is waiting."

They walked into the Mellow Mushroom and were seated at a high-top table. The waitress brought menus and asked what they wanted to drink. "I'll have a beer and what do you want, Tommy?"

"I'll have a Dr. Pepper."

"Really? I like that, Tommy. You show originality by making a different choice than most." The drinks were served, and Edward and Tommy decided on a meat lover's pizza with all the toppings with breadsticks.

Edward started texting on his phone, and Tommy questioned who he was talking to. Edward looked up and said, "Let's let your sister join in on the fun."

"I have plans for her too." Edward texted Katie and said, "I've got Tommy. I would suggest you meet us at Crater Lake at 7 pm if you don't want any accidents to happen. I warned you, Katie. Now you will know I am serious."

Katie heard the sound of the text and picked up her phone and started shaking. Immediately, Marta was called and was advised what Edward's plans were.

"Marta, I am supposed to come alone or he will hurt Tommy. I don't know what to do. I have got to go." Marta paused and gave some thought to what Katie wanted to do.

Finally she answered, "If you go, I will make sure that you are protected and that Edward can't hurt you. What time are you supposed to meet him and Tommy?"

"At 7:30 pm."

"Then, you have one hour before you have to be there. I will also contact the judge about getting a warrant out for your husband. One way or another, Edward is 'going down' tonight."

"I hope so," said Katie.

"I know how he gets and I know how quickly he can snap. He frightens me."

"Katie, you have got to stay strong! That is the only way you are going to get through this."

"I'll try. For Tommy's sake, I'll try."

Katie's mother called as she was talking to Marta and Katie told Marta she would call her back. Helen spoke in a concerned manner. "Katie, I have not understood why Edward started being so chummy with Tommy until now. He would not listen to me."

Katie lied and said reassuringly, "I know. Mom, it will be alright. Maybe he did want to take him fishing. Maybe we are misjudging him."

"I don't understand, Katie, and you are not fooling me. I know you well enough to know when something is wrong."

"I am going to meet them, mom. One way or another, all this drama will be over soon."

Ricardo got a call from Glenda that his brother and wife would be coming to visit this weekend. Glenda asked lovingly, "When will you be back? You have been gone for 3 weeks, and the baby is growing rapidly. I want you to feel the baby kick. He is really active!"

Ricardo said, "If he's anything like me, he will continue to be active but hopefully he will make better decisions than I did."

"Ricardo, I hope he will be just as sweet as you are." Ricardo smiled and said, "Spoken by my pregnant wife. Why did you fall in love with me, Glenda? You had every reason to doubt me."

Glenda paused and thought for a minute, then she answered, "Because sometimes I see that scared little boy in you, and I want him to know that he can finally feel loved and safe."

"Wow, Glenda, you are really something. You never give up or get mad at me."

Glenda said reassuringly, "There are times I get upset but I can't stay mad at you. I forgive you, and that's that."

Ricardo said, "I am coming home. Please call my brother and tell him that I will be home in a couple of days."

"I will! Then we can have a welcome home party. Your brother said that he has a proposition to talk to you about. He says it is something important that you might be interested in."

"Hmm, did he say what proposition he was talking about?" "Did he give you any idea what he might have meant?"

"No, Ricardo. He said he wanted to talk to you privately about it."

"Well, I'm curious what it is. After all these years, I will see my baby brother. I can't even imagine what he looks like."

"I'll see you soon. Be careful coming back."

"I have gone through tougher times and survived, Glenda. Nothing will keep me away from you and our baby."

Glenda got the house ready for Ricardo's arrival and flung her arms around him as he came through the door. "Ricardo! I am so glad you're here! Let me get you a drink!"

Ricardo put his suitcase down, ran into her arms, and hugged her tenderly. "Missed you, Glenda. You would not believe what happened on this job. It took a while, but I got Edward's money back and his jewels!"

"Edward's happy that he got his things back, but I'm happier."
"Happier?"
"Yes, I got you back and I get to meet your brother and his wife. They are coming tomorrow morning."

"Then I have time to find out about you and what is happening with the baby."

"I never thought I could be so happy!" His strong arms embraced Glenda and kissed her passionately and aggressively.

Ricardo looked at Glenda in a "suggestive manner" and said, "We have some catching up to do."

"I made your favorite Orange Chicken with new potatoes."

Ricardo took a whiff and rolled back his head in delight. "It smells heavenly."

Let me help you set the table, light some candles, and turn on some soft jazz. He played some *George Benson* music and danced Glenda around the kitchen. As Ricardo held Glenda in his arms, he said, "Now I'm home!" Passionate kisses and Latin dance moves filled the night with excitement and romance.

Joey called and said his flight would be arriving at 3:30 and asked if Ricardo and Glenda could meet him and his wife at the airport. Ricardo was nervous about seeing his brother, but all fear left when he saw his little brother and wife leaving the terminal and heading downstairs towards the baggage claim.

Ricardo stared in wonder at the little boy that had grown up before his eyes that was wearing a suit and expensive Italian leather shoes.

Joey's wife was shapely and taut wearing a revealing Paris fashion that showed off her best attributes.

Joey smiled and gave Ricardo a hug and introduced his wife Janie. Ricardo introduced Glenda and showed off her large pregnant stomach.

Proudly Joey said, "There is nothing like children. We have three of our own, and our oldest is graduating from high school this year."

Ricardo looked lovingly at Glenda and said, "Joey, I just had to find the right one. Good things are worth waiting for."

Janie laughed and gave a seductive and sweet grin to Ricardo. Janie said, "I bet you are a charmer. Joey has told me a lot about you."

Coyly Ricardo remarked, "Hopefully he left something out."

Joey decided to change the subject and said, "So was your boss impressed with your bank work?"

Ricardo spoke in a puzzled manner and said, "The boss said to leave all my findings at his place. He said he had some 'personal business to attend to."

Joey said, "I wonder what that was? We have got to catch up, Ricardo, and if you are interested I have a proposition for you that I think you might want to give some thought."

"You have got me curious, Joey. What do you think I might be interested in?"

Suddenly, Joey looked Ricardo in the eye and said, "You and I are not so different but you ended up on the wrong side of the tracks."

"How would you like to do the same type of work but for the good guys this time? Something where you can make an honest living?"

Ricardo pondered the suggestion and said, "I might be interested. Tell me more."

Chapter 32

Joey smiled coyly and said, "Janie, why don't you and Glenda get something to drink in the lounge, and Ricardo and I will get the luggage?"

"Sounds good to me." Janie walked towards the lounge, swaying her hips seductively from side to side. Then she turned around and looked at Glenda. "Coming Glenda? I can't wait to hear how Ricardo, the mystery man, met you. This calls for a glass of white wine."

Glenda spoke with reservation and concern in her voice and said, "I will tell you, but I doubt if you will believe me."

Glenda walked with Janie towards the lounge and opened the door in the direction of the bar. Janie looked Glenda in the eye and said, "Try me. I bet nothing beats the way I met Joey. Believe me that it was not love at first sight."

Glenda sat down at the bar and shyly said, "It was love at first sight for me. I just didn't know he felt the same way."

Janie sat down next to Glenda and said, "It is during the worst of times that they finally tell you. Did he ever tell you about his family at Chernobyl? Did he tell you what happened to his mom and dad? Do you know what special skills he has?"

Glenda looked down at the floor and said, "I was told not to ask and just to trust."

"Glenda, it is time you learn how to trust Ricardo and get more insight into his work."

"Janie, I know you are trying to help, but I would rather not know. I would rather let him do what he needs to do and just trust him."

Janie ordered white wine, and Glenda ordered a sprite. Janie was handed her glass of wine and waited for Glenda to be given her sprite.

Janie lifted up her glass and said, "A toast to the trusting wives of our unsung heroes. May they be around for a long time? Their adventures make our lives interesting."

Glenda clicked Janie's glass and said, "I wouldn't have it any other way."

Joey and Ricardo waited by the baggage claim area for Joey's and Jane's bags.

"So are you planning to continue this foolishness working for Edward till you get caught?" Joey said inquisitively.

"Do I have a choice? Glenda is going to be having our baby and I have got to take care of her." The bags came through, and Joey and Ricardo immediately picked them up.

As they walked towards the lounge, Joey said, "Yes, you do Ricardo. Courtesy of Chernobyl, I was given special skills and powers that have proved useful for the government. When you left, our stepparents raised me to have the finest education and helped me to understand the importance of patriotism for this country. I applied for a government operative job with the FBI and I got it. I am working with a special task force to stop terrorists that invade this country. We could work together, and you will be amazed how well you will get paid. I had to have surgery on my heart and with the new technology my heart is better than it was before."

The health benefits and 401K are better than anywhere else. "What kind of healthcare and 401K do you have?"

Ricardo looked at Joey and said sarcastically, "I have the assurance that if I work for him me and my family won't turn up dead."

Joey shook his head and said, "Wow! That's quite a retirement plan. Are you sure that is what you want?"

"No, and with this "personal business" he has got to deal with I am not sure what is going to happen but I know I don't want to be in the middle of it."

Joey said in a consoling tone, "I will make all the arrangements. All you have to do is say 'yes' and we can work together in Special Forces."

Ricardo started thinking about Marta and Vladimir and how they wanted him to work with them.

"Wouldn't Marta be surprised if I was actually working on her side? Okay, if you can make the arrangements I will consider your offer."

Edward drove into the parking lot next to Crater Lake and said, "Tommy, I have a little surprise for you. I found a good fishing spot near the caves where you can catch some big fish. Nobody knows about this spot but me."

"That sounds cool Edward. Where is it?" Edward got out of the truck, shut the door, and walked over to Tommy's passenger side door.

"Tommy, to find my fishing spot you have got to walk for a while. Are you up to it?" "I can walk, Edward. How far do we need to walk?"

"Just around the edge of the lake. I'll let you know when we get there." Tommy opened the truck door, got out, and closed the door, and followed Edward with fishing rods, tackle box, and backpack.

Edward carried a couple of camping chairs, tools, and supplies and led the way. Edward led Tommy on an uneven trail and remembered where his surprise for Tommy was hidden.

Tommy unexpectedly walked over the soft ground and fell into a large hole near the lake. Tommy fell five feet down in the direction of the caves and said in a terrified voice, "Edward help me! I think I sprained my ankle!"

Edward looked down into the large dirt man-made hole and said, "Your sister should have never crossed me. Let me see if she can find you now!"

Tommy cried, "Edward, why did you do this? Help me up!"

Edward said, viciously, "You wanted to fish Tommy? Well, if your sister does not come and get you then in the morning fish will find you, and I will use you for bait!"

Tommy said in a frightened voice, "Where is my sister? What have you done to Katie?"

"Nothing yet Tommy, but if she does not come back she is going to join you in a fish paradise."

Edward laughed sarcastically when he heard the groans and cries from his nephew.

"I can't believe you are so gullible that you fell for this!" Edward looked at his watch and called Katie on his cellphone.

Katie's phone rang, and the shuddering sound of Edward's voice could be heard on the other side of the phone. "Come on Katie. Come to the lake. Your brother is waiting for you."

As the echo of the phone hit the floor, it brought clearly into Katie's focus what Edward was trying to do to manipulate her. Edward said in a loud boisterous, mocking tone, "Katie, Katie, I know you're there. Come out, come out wherever you are. Your brother is such a crybaby you should see him now!"

Katie could hear moans and screams that were coming from a distance. Slowly raising the phone to her ear, thoughts of Tommy as a toddler flashed through her mind.

Anger, rage, and flames of adrenaline shot through her bloodstream as she thought about what Edward was putting her trusting little brother through, "What have you done with Tommy? You better not have hurt him or I'll..."

Sarcastically Edward said, "What will you do? It's your fault that he is here. If you had not run away he would be safe with your mom. By the way, your mom is next! Ha! Ha! You thought you could put one over on me. Guess again!"

"Please Edward, don't hurt him. You are mad at me, not him. Leave him alone. It's me that you want."

"Finally, you are seeing it my way. Get your butt down here Katie. We're waiting and don't try anything smart. Come alone if you care about your brother."

The phone went click, and then the sound of a dial tone rang through Katie's ears. Katie sat down and cried, "Tommy! Why Tommy? He hasn't hurt anyone!"

Katie called Marta and told her what Edward had said, "Good! Now I know the location, and the FBI will be all over this one." "Please Marta. He will kill Tommy if I don't do what he says."

"Katie, he might kill him anyway and you too. Are you willing to let me help you?"

"Yes. Please help me. I don't know what to do."

"Then trust me that I will make sure you and Tommy are safe. I give you my word of honor. He won't even know we are there but you need to do what I say. It's for your own good."

"I am willing to listen. Do you have a plan? Yes, but I am going to need you to be the distraction. Pretend you are going to do what he says and we will take it from there."

Katie said hesitantly, "How will I know where you are?"

Marta replied, "You won't. Just trust that I will be close at hand, and this is the last day of Edward's tirades and threats. He won't know what hit him."

Katie made a deep breathing sound and said, "I hope you are right. No one has caught him yet."

Marta said, "Time is wasting. It's time to go to Crater Lake. Are you sure you are up to this?"

"If it will save my brother, I will do anything."

"Talk to you soon, Katie." Katie drove towards Crater Lake and relived the scenarios in her mind of Edward's anger and rage that had been experienced during their marriage.

Tearfully Katie said to herself, "I hope I make it in time. God please let my brother be alright.

The sound of the crashing waves against the beach reminded her that she was close to where Edward took Tommy. The caverns had not changed since she visited them with Edward years ago. The car turned into the parking lot, Katie got out, and locked the door behind her. Her footsteps and the crashing waves were the only sound that could be heard as she walked towards the caverns. "Edward, I'm here. Where are you?" Katie continued to call Edward's name until she suddenly felt the presence of someone standing behind her.

A cold unfeeling voice said, "Good evening Katie. It's been a long time." Katie started shaking and trembling as she slowly began to turn around and look in the face of a possible killer and psycho.

Marta contacted Vladimir and advised him to come to Crater Lake with a special task force so Edward could be caught in the act.

Vladimir called agents from the unit that were skilled in dealing with dangerous combat situations and could be called in a moment's notice. Joey got a call on his cellphone and was told that his help would be needed this evening to do a special assignment.

Joey advised that he was without a vehicle and that he would not be able to help. Ricardo overheard Joey's side of the conversation and asked if he needed a ride somewhere. Joey advised that his mission was top secret and that he needed to go to headquarters.

"I'll drive you to FBI headquarters. No problem. What do they want you to do?" "I can't talk about it because my work is classified."

"I understand so I will drive you. Glenda, I will leave you here to entertain Jane while we are gone."

"Ok Ricardo. We'll be here." Joey gave Jane a kiss and followed Ricardo to the car. Ricardo opened the car door and opened the door for Joey.

As they were alone in the car, Ricardo said, "Do you need help Joey? I might be good at catching bad guys because I was considered a bad guy myself at one point."

"I might, but you are going to need to keep hidden till I need you." "No problem bro. This will be like old times."

"Not quite Ricardo. Each assignment is like a game of Russian roulette. You don't know if this might be your last assignment, but you go because you like to be a part of the action."

Ricardo's mind drifted back to the first time he encountered being this close to the FBI. He had been taken in for interrogation, knocked out, and put in a hospital room that looked like something out of a murder mystery novel. When the realization overcame him that something was wrong, it was too late. Marta and Vladimir permanently changed his facial features.

What would Joey do if he knew what his big brother had been doing all these years? Ricardo's car pulled into the parking lot, and Joey got out. Ricardo started to get out of the car as he saw Vladimir and some other agents walking towards the building. "This must be some of those Special Forces," and Joey will be one of them. Joey went inside, and Ricardo peered into the window to get a better look at what was going on.

Vladimir was leading the agents towards a call to action and the agents followed his call and stood on their feet. Joey stood beside Vladimir and talked to the men and women that had come to help. Ricardo wondered who was so important that Joey and the other top agents were called in for a secret mission until he saw on the screen the face of his boss and enemy, Edward.

Ricardo shook his head and said, "*Something is going down tonight. My question is whose side should I be on? My brother's or the man who pays me a good income?*"

Ricardo reasoned with himself about what would be the right thing to do. "*Edward had given him money, position, women, and any material pleasure a man would want. Edward had seen potential in him and helped teach skills that made him appear charming, powerful, and in control at all times. There was an emptiness that people or things could not fill even though he never wanted for anything bought, sold, or stolen. Those feelings were kept inside, so he did not have to feel bad or guilty. He could still remember his father's words and his mother's loving correction when he chooses wrong over right. I wonder what they would think of me now. Why didn't I stay with my brother? Why did I let Edward talk me into a life of crime?*"

The cell phone rang, and Ricardo noticed a surprising but familiar number. "Hello? How are you doing? I can't say I am surprised to hear from you."

The voice on the other side of the phone said, "Ricardo, I need your help. Edward has crossed the line this time, and you are the only person he will acknowledge. Can you give me a hand to stop him?"

Ricardo paused and contemplated what would be the best answer to give. After a long pause, Ricardo said, "I'm listening to you, Marta. What do you want me to do?"

"I want you to scout out where Edward has taken Tommy but be incognito where he can't see you. Katie is afraid that her brother is hurt and does not know where Edward has hidden him."

Ricardo listened and said, "I am at the FBI station with my brother, and I need to find out if he needs a ride."

Curiously, Katie said, "Who is your brother? I had heard a secret agent from another state was coming, but I didn't hear about your brother being here. Come to think of it; I didn't know you had a brother."

Sarcastically, Ricardo said, "Believe it or not, yes I have a brother. His name is Joey, and he is your secret agent."

It's a small world, Ricardo. Everything is going full circle for you." "It's hard to believe, but I am in touch with my family again." "Ricardo, will you help?"

"Yes, I will message Joey that I will be at the lake and to ask his co-workers if he could get a ride with them."

Ricardo started texting Joey about his plans and waited for affirmation from his brother. Ricardo got a thumbs up notification on his cell phone and advised Marta what Joey had texted him. "Meet me at Crater Lake in 15 minutes but make sure that Edward doesn't see you. He doesn't know that you are helping Katie."

Reassuringly, Ricardo said, "Don't worry. Edward will never suspect that I am looking for Tommy, but you must promise that you don't blow my cover."

"I promise Ricardo as long as you help no one will know you were even there."

Ricardo drove to Crater Lake, got out of the car, and found that he blended into the beach scenery. Ricardo remembered the wrath and anger Edward had and trembled at the thought of being discovered by him. He walked softly to avoid being discovered and breaking his cover. The sounds of a teenager screaming out for help could be heard echoing through the caverns.

Katie looked at Edward and said, "Edward what have you done to Tommy? He has done nothing to you."

"We were just having a little talk and he fell into the caverns."

"Please help me get him out. Edward, please don't hurt him. Take me but don't hurt my brother."

"Why should I listen to you when you ran away from me?"

"I'm back now Edward. Please help Tommy up so we can go home." "Is this what it takes to get your attention, Katie?"

Tommy could hear Katie and cried, "Katie, you're walking into a trap. Katie watch out!"

"Be quiet or your sister will be joining you! On second thought, what is one more thing to get rid of?"

Edward ran towards Katie, took her by the throat, and pinned her to the ground. "This is the last time you will ever mess with me! I'm sick of you!"

Edward's angry and unsettling eyes had a twinge of hate, revenge, and retribution. "Edward, you're hurting me! I can't breathe." Edward looked angrily in her eyes as he had his hands around her neck.

Marta signaled to Joey and the other agents to come in for the kill and stop Edward. A voice could be heard from a close distance that said, "Stop in the name of the law."

Edward turned around, and there was no one there. He let go of Katie, got up, and felt a sharp punch to his cheek. "Who did that? Show your face!"

Marta walked out from behind a hill and said, "It's over, Edward. You're going to jail."

Edward said, "Get away." This is none of your business." A voice from the shadows said, "I'll make it my business!"

Joey pushed Edward down and slugged him in the jaw. Edward got his gun out of his pocket, clicked the cylinder of the magnum in his hand, and prepared to shoot.

Ricardo saw Edward pull a gun in the direction of Joey and became incognito so Edward would not see him. The gun was taken from his hand, and a loud gunshot could be heard as the gun hit the ground. Marta and the other agents were busy fighting with Edward and his men, so Ricardo jumped into the water and swam towards the caverns where Tommy was. Tommy was unconscious, leaning against the cave wall.
Ricardo rescued him and brought him to the land. When he got back, Joey had Edward in handcuffs and said that he would be in jail for a long time. Edward said, "No one can keep me behind bars, and I will find you."

Joey smiled, slugged him to the ground, and said, "Good, I'll be waiting."

"Katie," Edward said empathically, "don't you know I love you? Why are you so hard to please?" Katie was shaking in fear as you turned to Edward and said, "I don't feel love when I look at you... only fear... You're a monster!" Edward clenched his teeth, looked at his bride defiantly and said, "There will be a woman who will be in my arms when I get out! Just wait and see." Joey read Edward his rights and put him in the back of the police vehicle. Katie stood in the same spot trembling with fear.

Marta walked over to her and hugged Katie as tears fell down her soft cheeks. "I really loved him. He took everything from me and then treated me like dirt. I don't understand. I thought if I loved him enough, if I gave enough, he would love me." Marla said in a calm but firm tone, "If he doesn't love you for the person you are, then giving or doing isn't going to help. People like him don't know how to love because they don't love themselves."

Ricardo carried Tommy in his arms, and Katie grasped at the cuts and bruises on him. "We have got to get him to a hospital!"

Marta called 911 dispatch and an ambulance was called. "Mercy hospital isn't that far and the ambulance is on its way."

Ricardo asked, "Is there anything else I can do to help?"

Marta said, "It's best if Edward does not know you were here. Thanks for your help."

Ricardo gave an arrogant grin and said, "Anytime Marta. I told you that you would not be able to forget me that easily." Marta gave a coy smile in Ricardo's direction and walked away.

Edward's mother called him as he got in the patrol car and wanted to know how he was. "Katie framed me mom, and the police are taking me to jail. I didn't do anything, but I am going to have to prove I'm not a violent person now. Yes, mom, I tried to make up with Katie. I did everything I could think of to win her love again. I am going to try to reason with her. Yes mom, goodbye."

"Edward, you are going to be in prison for a long time. You have a long laundry list of crimes."

"Who are you? Your voice sounds familiar."

A familiar face turned around and said, "Surprise Edward! It's Vladimir. Edward said disgustingly; "I should have knocked you both off when I had the chance."

"Marta and I have come a long way with the FBI since we started. We have always made a good team."

Edward angrily said, "That is till Ricardo comes around, and you know you will never be Ricardo to her."

Vladimir said, "Shut him up before I do. I have had more than I can stand just hearing him for a short while. I don't know how Katie put up with you."

"She loved me like I can get every woman to love me. Katie is just one of the many women I have had, it's just that I married her."

165

Chapter 33

Vladimir and Joey led Edward into the interrogation room.

"Now this can go easy on you, or we can throw the book at you. Who helped you find Katie? I tapped her phone because I had to know where she was. I could have gotten to her sooner, but I waited till she would come home and forget this foolishness. I gave her everything, a home, a camp, and all that a man could give."

"Yes, Edward, you gave her everything. Everything but the love and security she needed."

Edward was taken to FBI headquarters for more questioning and said that he would not say anything without his attorney. Joey left Edward with Vladimir in the interrogation room and proceeded to walk outside and call Ricardo. Ricardo picked up the phone and recognized the number.

Ricardo said, "So Joey, what is happening with Edward?"

Joey said reassuringly, "Vladimir has it in for Edward, so don't be surprised if he doesn't come back anytime soon to give you a new assignment. Can you pick me up in a half-hour?"

"Of course! I'll see you soon. I have been thinking about your proposition, I mean, what is going to happen to me if Edward is locked up? Will I end up in prison too?"

Joey said, "You work with me, and I'll see what I can do for you."

Glenda was calling on the other line, so Ricardo said he would talk to him later. "Hello Glenda, what's up?"

"Not much; it's just that Jane has been filling me in on you. When are you coming home?"

"In about an hour because Joey is hard at work helping to throw out the garbage and clean up at his work. Glenda laughed as she looked at their garage."

"Maybe Joey can give you some tips on not being a packrat."

Ricardo was slightly amused but pretended not to show it. "Very funny Glenda. My garage shows my taste in tools, hardware, and hobbies. Anything you can think of can be found in the garage or attic, so nothing is really lost."

Ricardo sat in the parking lot of the FBI building and waited for Joey. His mind traveled back to the day he met Marta and held her in his arms. "Whatever happened to Marta? You and I could have made it."

Memories of warm embraces and nights of passion flashed through his mind, and feelings of regret and sadness filled his heart. "Marta..."

The sound of footsteps could be heard approaching the car. Joey opened the passenger door, got in, and closed the car door. Joey smiled at his brother and said, "I know that it was fun while it lasted Ricardo, but eventually all of us have to grow up and make an honest living."

Ricardo started up the car and said, "What makes you think you are different from me? You use your special abilities just like I do."

Joey grinned and said, "The difference is that all your crimes are going against you in a court of law. What I do is done on the side of the good guys. Your life will catch up with you, but I will retire with a 401K and stocks to my name."

"Good point Joey! So, when do I start, and what will be my first assignment?" "Do you mean it, Ricardo? That means you will have to be a double agent."

"No problem. I feel like I have had to play both sides of the law for so long that I have plenty of experience."

"Good! That experience will come in handy. Let's go home and get some dinner. I know two good-looking women that are waiting for us!"

"Wait till I tell Glenda I'll be working with you. She will be thrilled!"

Joey listened to a song on the radio and said, "Don't expect the work to be easy. You earn respect in this business, and it does not come quickly."

Ricardo drove into the driveway of his suburban home and said, "I would expect nothing less."

The End

"Till the Final Goodnight" (Ricardo's Song) Played with guitar
By Kathy Lou Waskett

G   Em7 Em   Am
Dearest Sweetheart, I love you, yes, I do.

C   D7

You know I'll always care for you. GEm7   Em   Am
But I must go. I'm sure you know, please don't cry. C   D7
Just one more kiss and then the final goodbye.

Chorus

B7   Em   Bm   E7

I knew when we met, I'd never regret Am   D7   G   B7
        Em
One sunrise, one sunset with you. B7   Em
But my journey takes a path,   Bm   E7
Known to very few, Am   D7   G   G
So I must bid you adieu.

G   Em7 Em   Am

Till that moment, think of a day
C   D7

When we'll marry and I'll take you away. G Em7   Em   Am
Until then let us dance I'll hold you tight. C D7
Just one more kiss, and then the final goodnight.

(Chorus)

"Show Me What Real Love Can Be" (Marta's Song)

Latin Tempo - Meant to be played with samba
instruments, guitar, and maracas By Kathy Lou Waskett
Am   Dm E7   Am Dm
E7 Am Dm E7

(Chorus)

Am   Dm   E7   Am Ohhh, how I long for
his love. Dm   E7   Am

Ohhh, how I long for his touch.

Dm   E7

Ohhh, how I long for you, Am   Dm   E7
To show me what real love can be.

He leads a double life, but I'm still his wife.

Dm   E7

He says it's for me to defend our liberty. Am   Dm E7
And as he flies away, I say just one more day. Am   Dm E7
Let him come safely home to me.

(Chorus)

I may never know the path he goes, Dm   E7
But he says it's for me to protect our family. Am   Dm E7
And as he flies away, I say just one more day. Am   Dm   E7
Let him come safely home to me.

(Chorus)